James Gould Cozzens

An Annotated Checklist

By Pierre Michel

Université de Liège, Belgium
Center for American Studies, Royal Library, Brussels

D1450739

The Kent State University Press

The Serif Series
Bibliographies and Checklists, Number 22

William White, General Editor
Wayne State University

Published simultaneously in Belgium
by the Center for American Studies,
Royal Library, Brussels

ISBN 0-87338-122-x
Library of Congress Catalog Card Number 75-169068
Printed in Belgium

Designed by Merald E. Wrolstad

First Edition

Contents

Preface

James Gould Cozzens is one of those literary phenomena such as can be produced only in America. In our days of noisy advertising and nationwide promotional campaigns, the man himself stands out as a remarkable exception to the rule that an author should, in a way, act as his own sales agent by appearing in public as often as he can. Cozzens rarely leaves his home in Williamstown, Massachusetts; he has never accepted writer-in-residence appointments, nor has he ever embarked on lecture tours. He has consistently refused to talk about his own work, and the tone and content of the only two interviews that he has ever granted leave many doubts as to whether one should take at face value the little information which they reveal about him. At a time when writers' lives, not unlike those of baseball stars, are expected to be made public and to become part of the national "literary" heritage, at a time when writers and artists pour forth written and spoken pronouncements on their craft or on political and social issues, Cozzens has remained uncommonly silent. Little has transpired by way of biographical information; the Cozzens papers at the Princeton University Library are not open to the public, and a biography of Cozzens is not likely to be written soon.

7

Cozzens also stands outside the well-trodden paths of contemporary American fiction. Except for one timid and not wholly successful attempt, he has shied away from the themes of alienation, rebellion, dissent, and protest now proliferating in American literature. Technical experimentation and the techniques of the absurd and of black humor are even more remote from his preoccupations. His America is small-town, eastern seaboard America, peopled with upper-middle-class professionals – lawyers and doctors, occasionally businessmen and high-ranking officers–whose main concern is the preservation of an order that is worth preserving for the simple reason that, so far, it has in their opinion held the community together to everyone's satisfaction. Some have argued that Cozzens' "philosophy of limits" is merely an encouragement to the defense of the status quo and that the views he dramatizes in his novels are at best conservative and at worst reactionary. Whatever one's stand, there is no denying that his fiction is a fiction of acceptance and of participation.

Public and critical recognition was a long time in coming for Cozzens. His first four novels, which his publisher no longer lists, went virtually unnoticed; his short stories had neither the technical virtuosity nor the "commitment" necessary to attract attention when they were published in the 1920s and 1930s. The novels which appeared between 1930 and 1940 received better reviews; *S.S. San Pedro*, *The Last Adam*, *Castaway*, and *Men and Brethren* (one may regard *Ask Me Tomorrow* as the sort of accident not infrequent in a writer's career) are technically highly accomplished pieces whose themes clearly foreshadow those of the "mature" novels. Given the obvious and sustained evolution of Cozzens' manner and themes toward his masterpiece, *Guard of Honor*, *Castaway*, a modern Robinson Crusoe tale mildly experimental in technique, is a surprise, and one may regret that Cozzens chose not to pursue this vein a little further. Critics only began to really acknowledge Cozzens in the 1940s, when *Guard of Honor*, his best artistic achievement, was awarded the Pulitzer Prize. Cozzens was then an established novelist, and critics began to take stock of his earlier fiction and to devote to it the attention that it deserved. Cozzens was at long last accepted as a novelist who, perhaps, had no spectacular solutions to propose for the evils of the world, but who said what he had to say in an unobtrusive, quiet way, in a subdued tone, whose style and sense of structure were brilliant, and whose philosophy appealed to a large section of the American reading public of the 1940s and 1950s.

The publication of *By Love Possessed* in 1957 caused an uproar whose echoes reverberated throughout the country and even abroad. It was acclaimed as a masterwork, hailed as the novel of the decade, even proposed for the Nobel Prize. At last, some critics sighed, American fiction was coming to its senses and Cozzens was going to rescue it from the mire in which it had been wallowing for too long. Others vehemently took the opposite view and accused Cozzens of all possible sins, literary and other. He was called a genius and a fraud at once, and much was said that was grossly exaggerated. But then, not only was the *By Love Possessed* affair the occasion for many critics to re-examine Cozzens' whole corpus of fiction and to discover its qualities, it also put him into a new perspective : here was a novelist who could no longer be ignored. Some of the most vociferous detractors of *By Love Possessed* admitted that some of his novels belonged to the best vein even though they consistently preferred to avoid fashionable topics. Serious critics accepted him as a curious phenomenon, but one worth looking into; books were written, scholarly papers were published, and Cozzens was taught at universities.

By Love Possessed sold extremely well, perhaps for reasons associated with the intellectual and political mood of the time, as John William Ward has explained. *Children and Others*, a collection of stories almost all written in the 1930s and *Morning Noon and Night* were published after the tumult over *By Love Possessed* had subsided and fared less well commercially. Many would certainly have wished for a return in *Morning Noon and Night* to the directness of *Guard of Honor* and for a departure from the style and stiffness of *By Love Possessed*. That Cozzens chose to persevere in his mannerisms is a measure of his intellectual integrity or, as some would say, of his lack of flexibility.

Cozzens wrote in the shadow of towering figures such as Faulkner and Hemingway, whose contemporary he was. Perhaps he should not be elevated to their ethereal heights, but he does not deserve to join the gallery of forgotten figures either. Scholarly criticism has shown that at least six of his novels are excellent fiction; a Pulitzer Prize, the Howells Medal of the American Academy of Arts and Letters, and the amount of critical attention his fiction has received bear testimony to this remarkable achievement.

The first section of this bibliography lists the first American and British editions of Cozzens' books, stories, essays and other nonfiction, and poems in chronological order. Secondary sources include books on Cozzens, criticism in books and periodicals, and the reviews of each of his books. This checklist includes British as well as American material, but there has been no systematic attempt to trace continental European material, though some items of particular significance have been included.

No bibliography can ever claim to be complete, but a bibliographer can take comfort in the knowledge that he has exhausted all the sources and possibilities available to him. The tracing of Cozzens' early short pieces of prose and poetry proved particularly difficult; written when Cozzens was unknown, they never found their way into the standard bibliographical listings, and Cozzens, though he was of very generous help in many other matters, was very reluctant to provide information about them. Ludwig's and Bracher's bibliographies, as well as Meriwether's for the dates of some first editions, were a reliable starting point. But they were far from complete and their lists of secondary sources stopped early. I am indebted to the Kent School, Kent, Connecticut, at which Cozzens was a student, for opening the files of *The Kent Quarterly* for me. This led to the discovery of a number of items heretofore unknown to critics. In 1969-1970 I was a frequent visitor to the Reference Desk of the Frost Library at Amherst College, Amherst, Massachusetts; the competence of its staff, Floyd Merritt and Mrs. Brown, and their patience with me were admirable. I also wish to thank Mrs. G. Lercangée, assistant director, and Mrs. G. Grootjans, librarian, at the Center for

American Studies, Royal Library, Brussels, Belgium, for their unfailing help. Finally, all this would not have been possible had I not been the fortunate recipient of an ACLS research fellowship in 1969-1970. Needless to say, I alone remain responsible for errors and omissions.

P. M.

Works of James Gould Cozzens

Books

A1   *Confusion.* Boston: B. J. Brimmer Co., 1924. 404 pp.

A2   *Michael Scarlett: A History.* New York: Albert & Charles Boni, October 1925. 318 pp. London: Robert Holden & Co., June 1927. 318 pp.

A3   *Cock Pit.* New York: William Morrow & Co., 1928. 302 pp.

A4   *The Son of Perdition.* New York: William Morrow & Co., August 22, 1929. 304 pp. London: Longmans, Green & Co., October 3, 1929. 304 pp.

A5   *S.S. San Pedro.* New York: Harcourt, Brace & Co., August 27, 1931. 136 pp. London: Longmans, Green & Co., September 10, 1931. 118 pp. First appeared in *Scribner's Magazine*, 88, No. 2 (August 1930), 113-128, 214-228.

A6   *The Last Adam.* New York: Harcourt, Brace & Co., January 5, 1933. 301 pp. Under title *A Cure of Flesh.* London: Longmans, Green & Co., February 23, 1933. 289 pp.

A7   *Castaway.* London: Longmans, Green & Co., September 27, 1934. 181 pp. New York: Random House, Inc., November 7, 1934. 181 pp.

A8 *Men and Brethren*. New York: Harcourt, Brace & Co.,
    January 2, 1936. 282 pp. London: Longmans,
    Green & Co., March 9, 1936. 309 pp.

A9 *Ask Me Tomorrow*. New York: Harcourt, Brace & Co.,
    June 13, 1940. 338 pp. London: Longmans, Green
    & Co., October 7, 1940. 318 pp.

A10 *The Just and the Unjust*. New York: Harcourt, Brace &
    Co., July 23, 1942. 434 pp. London: Jonathan
    Cape, Ltd., April 12, 1943. 319 pp.

A11 *Guard of Honor*. New York: Harcourt, Brace & Co.,
    September 30, 1948. 631 pp. London: Longmans,
    Green & Co., November 7, 1949. 631 pp.

A12 *By Love Possessed*. New York: Harcourt, Brace & Co.,
    August 26, 1957. 570 pp. London: Longmans,
    Green & Co., April 14, 1958. 570 pp.

A13 *Children and Others*. New York: Harcourt, Brace &
    World, October 7, 1964. 343 pp. London:
    Longmans, Green & Co., April 5, 1965. 343 pp.
    Contains B25, B22, B24, B21, B23, B8, B9, B11,
    B29, B26, B28, B16, B14, B15, B13, and two
    heretofore unpublished stories, "King Midas Has
    Ass's Ears" and "Eyes to See."

A14 *Morning Noon and Night*. New York: Harcourt, Brace
    & World, August 26, 1968. 408 pp. London:
    Longmans, Green & Co., January 27, 1969.
    408 pp.

Stories in periodicals

B1 "Religion for Beginners: A Nova Scotian Sketch."
Kent Quarterly, 14, No. 1 (December 1921), 25-28.

B2 "Remember the Rose." *Harvard Advocate*, 109, No. 9
(June 1, 1923), 395-397. Reprinted in Donald Hall,
ed. *The Harvard Advocate Anthology*. New York:
Twayne Publishers, 1950, pp. 217-223 and
Freeport, N.Y.: Books for Libraries Press, 1970,
pp. 217-223.

B3 "Abishag." *Linonia*, 1, No. 2 (June 1925), 45-53.

B4 "A Letter to a Friend." *Pictorial Review*, 27, No. 8
(May 1926), 16, 116, 117.

B5 "Future Assured." *Saturday Evening Post*, 202, No. 18
(November 2, 1929), 22-23, 116, 120-121, 124.

B6 "The Defender of Liberties." *Alhambra*, 1, No. 4
(January 1930), 14-17, 54-56.

B7 "Lions Are Lower Today." *Saturday Evening Post*, 202,
No. 33 (February 15, 1930), 36, 38, 40, 154, 158.

B8 "Some Day You'll Be Sorry." *Saturday Evening Post*,
202, No. 51 (June 21, 1930), 44, 47, 60, 63-64, 66.
Reprinted in A13.

B9 "We'll Recall It With Affection." *Saturday Evening Post*,
203, No. 14 (October 4, 1930), 12-13, 149-150,
152-154. Reprinted in A13.

B10 "October Occupancy." *American Magazine*, 110, No. 4
      (October 1930), 56-59, 153-158.

B11 "The Guns of the Enemy." *Saturday Evening Post*, 203,
      No. 18 (November 1, 1930), 12-13, 74, 77-78, 80,
      82. Reprinted in A13.

B12 "Fortune and Men's Eyes." *Woman's Home Companion*,
      58, No. 2 (February 1931), 29-30, 134, 136, 138,
      140.

B13 "Farewell to Cuba." *Scribner's Magazine*, 90, No. 5
      (November 1931), 533-544. Reprinted in A13.

B14 "The Way to Go Home." *Saturday Evening Post*, 204,
      No. 26 (December 26, 1931), 12-13, 59-60.
      Reprinted in A13.

B15 "Every Day's a Holiday." *Scribner's Magazine*, 94,
      No. 6 (December 1933), 339-344. Reprinted in A13.

B16 "My Love to Marcia." *Collier's*, 93, No. 9 (March 3,
      1934), 16-17, 46-47. Reprinted in A13.

B17 "Love Leaves Town." *American Magazine*, 118, No. 3
      (September 1934), 24-27, 119-121.

B18 "Straight Story." *Collier's*, 94, No. 20 (November 17,
      1934), 22.

B19 "Success Story." *Collier's*, 95, No. 16 (April 20, 1935),
      26.

B20 "Foot in It." *Redbook Magazine*, 65, No. 4 (August
      1935), 28-29. Reprinted under title "Clerical Error"
      in Ellery Queen, ed. *The Literature of Crime*. Boston:
      Little, Brown & Co., 1950, pp. 376-379. Under

title "Clerical Error" in *Contemporary American Short Stories*, Huebers Fremdsprachliche Texte, No. 101, München. Max Hueber Verlag, n.d., pp. 13-16.

B21 "Total Stranger." *Saturday Evening Post*, 208, No. 33 (February 15, 1936), 8-9, 96, 98, 100. Reprinted in Leo Hamalian and Edmond L. Volpe, eds. *Pulitzer Prize Reader*. New York: Popular Library, 1961, pp. 213-227. Reprinted in A13.

B22 "Whose Broad Stripes and Bright Stars." *Saturday Evening Post*, 208, No. 47 (May 23, 1936), 16-17, 69, 71. Reprinted in A13.

B23 "Something About a Dollar." *Saturday Evening Post*, 209, No. 7 (August 15, 1936), 27-28, 62, 64. Reprinted in A13.

B24 "The Animals' Fair." *Saturday Evening Post*, 209, No. 29 (January 16, 1937), 18-19, 47, 50, 53-54. Reprinted in A13.

B25 "Child's Play." *Saturday Evening Post*, 209, No. 33 (February 13, 1937), 16-17, 61, 63, 65. Reprinted in A13.

B26 "Men Running." *Atlantic Monthly*, 160, No. 1 (July 1937), 81-91. Reprinted in Katharine M. Jones, ed. *New Confederate Short Stories*. Columbia: University of South Carolina Press, 1960, pp. 12-31. Reprinted in A13.

B27 "Son and Heir." *Saturday Evening Post*, 210, No. 40 (April 2, 1938), 10-11, 86, 88-89, 91.

B28 "One Hundred Ladies." *Saturday Evening Post*, 237,
No. 26 (July 11-18, 1964), 40, 42-43, 45-47.
Reprinted in A13.

B29 *"Candida* by Bernard Shaw." *Saturday Evening Post*,
237, No. 27 (July 25-August 1, 1964), 50, 52, 54,
57. Reprinted in A13.

Essays and other nonfiction

C1 "A Democratic School." *Atlantic Monthly*, 125, No. 3 (March 1920), 383-384. Reprinted under title "In Defense of Boarding Schools," *Kent Quarterly*, 12, No. 2 (March 1920), 50-52.

C2 "The Trail of the Lakes." *Kent Quarterly*, 12, No. 3 (May 1920), 86-91.

C3 "A Friendly Thinker." *Kent Quarterly*, 13, No. 1 (December 1920), 13-14.

C4 "Good Old Main Street." *Kent Quarterly*, 13, No. 2 (March 1921), 40-42.

C5 "A Study in the Art of the Novel." *Kent Quarterly*, 14, No. 4 (July 1922), 77-79.

C6 Review of Joseph Hergesheimer's *The Bright Shawl*. *Harvard Advocate*, 109, No. 3 (December 1, 1922), 85-86.

C7 Review of Lord Dunsany's *Don Rodriguez: Chronicles of Shadow Valley*. *Harvard Advocate*, 109, No. 4 (January 1, 1923), 120-121.

C8 Review of Jane Austen's *Love and Freindship*. *Harvard Advocate*, 109, No. 7 (April 7, 1923), 291.

C9 "The Point of View." *Kent Quarterly*, 17, No. 3 (June 1925), 55-59.

C10 "What You Should Know about the Club Library." *Winged Foot*, 38, No. 9 (September 1927), 29-30.

C11 "Notes from the Club Library." *Winged Foot*, 38, No. 10 (October 1927), 17.

C12 "The Library Talk for the Month." *Winged Foot*, 38, No. 11 (November 1927), 28-29.

C13 "Notes from the Club Library." *Winged Foot*, 38, No. 12 (December 1927), 42.

C14 "Notes from the Club Library." *Winged Foot*, 39, No. 1 (January 1928), 20-21.

C15 "Thoughts Brought on by 633 Manuscripts." *Bookman*, 73, No. 4 (June 1931), 381-384.

C16 Introduction to *Balzac's Masterpieces. Ten Novels by Honoré de Balzac.* Philadelphia: David McKay Co., 1931, pp. IX-XII.

C17 "Kent, A New School." *Town and Country*, 88, No. 4109 (August 1, 1933), 38-41, 57.

C18 Foreword to *Kent Quarterly*, 1, No. 1 (November 26, 1936), [3]-4.

C19 Review of Oliver La Farge's *The Eagle in the Egg. New York Times Book Review*, July 24, 1949, pp. 1, 17.

C20 "Notes on a Difficulty of Law by One Unlearned in it." *Bucks County Law Reporter*, 1 (1951), 302-306.

C21 "FHS–A Faith That did not Fail." Program of celebration of the fiftieth year of Kent School, Kent, Connecticut, 1956, pp. [6-9]. Also appears in *Fifty Years, 1906-1956, Kent School.* Published by the Committee for Kent School's fiftieth anniversary, 1956, pp. 113-115.

C22 Review of Arthur Koestler's *Reflections on Hanging. Harvard Law Review*, 71, No. 7 (May 1958), 1377-1381.

Poetry

D1 "The Andes." *Quill*, 30, No. 3 (January 1915), 5.

D2 "The Trust in Princes." *Harvard Advocate*, 109, No. 2 (November 1, 1922), 44. Reprinted in *Kent Quarterly*, 15, No. 1 (January 1923), 8.

D3 "Where Angels Fear to Tread." *Harvard Advocate*, 109, No. 3 (December 1, 1922), 86.

D4 "The Passing." *Harvard Advocate*, 109, No. 4 (January 1, 1923), 121.

D5 "Condolence." *Harvard Advocate*, 109, No. 5 (February 1, 1923), 151. Reprinted in Donald Hall, ed. *The Harvard Advocate Anthology*. New York: Twayne Publishers, 1950, pp. 216-217 and Freeport, N.Y.: Books for Libraries Press, 1970, pp. 216-217.

D6 "The Virginia Rose: A Ballad for Eunice." *Harvard Advocate*, 109, No. 8 (May 1, 1923), 338-339.

D7 "Two Arts." *Harvard Advocate*, 109, No. 8 (May 1, 1923), 347.

D8 "For a Motet by Josquin de Pres." *Harvard Advocate*, 109, No. 9 (June 1, 1923), 404.

D9 "Romanesque." *Kent Quarterly*, 15, No. 4 (July 1923), 85.

D10 "ΑΦΡΟΛΙΤΗΚΥΠΡΙΑ." *Kent Quarterly*, 15, No. 4 (July 1923), 91.

D11 "The Long Elusion." *Casements*, July 1923. [Published
by students of Brown University, Providence, R.I.,
from January 1923 to January 1925. Np.]

D12 "Hail and Farewell." *Harvard Advocate*, 110, No. 1
(October 1, 1923), 13.

D13 "Blue Seas." *Palms*, 1, No. 4 (Autumn 1923), 110.

Secondary sources
Books on James Gould Cozzens

A1 Bracher, Frederick. *The Novels of James Gould Cozzens*.
New York: Harcourt, Brace & Co., 1959. 306 pp.,
biblio., index.

The first detailed book-length study of Cozzens' themes and
techniques. Discusses all the novels through *By Love Possessed*
but devotes little attention to the stories. Carefully traces
Cozzens' evolution, particularly from *S.S. San Pedro* on. Bracher
is at his best on *Guard of Honor*, especially in his analysis of the
structure of the novel. Though coming in the immediate wake
of the furor over *By Love Possessed*, this study does not take a
stand either for or against the novel but follows a middle course
that hedges on critical appreciation, especially as regards style,
and makes no effort to mention, much less denounce, Cozzens'
"mannerisms" and prejudices.

A2 Hicks, Granville. *James Gould Cozzens*. University of
Minnesota Pamphlets on American Writers, No. 58.
Minneapolis: University of Minnesota Press, 1966.
47 pp., biblio.

A concise, chronological introduction to Cozzens' writings
through *Children and Others*. Hicks devotes two-thirds of his text
to an analysis of the themes of the novels and the last third to
an explanation of what makes Cozzens' fiction "traditional" (his
preference for the upper-middle class, his disinterest in social
questions, his handling of minorities, his ignorance of emotions).

23

Hicks makes little effort to assess the novels critically; he devotes one paragraph to *Children and Others*, whose stories, except for "Eyes to See," he finds slick.

A3 Maxwell, D. E. S. *Cozzens*. Writers and Critics Series, No. 35. Edinburgh and London: Oliver and Boyd, 1964. 119 pp., biblio.

An excellent and fluently written introduction that concentrates on Cozzens' "philosophy" and technique. Maxwell's analysis of Cozzens' narrative technique is remarkable, but he is not critical enough of the style of *By Love Possessed*. His treatment is chronological and traces Cozzens' development from *Cock Pit* to *By Love Possessed* (and therefore does not cover *Confusion*, *Michael Scarlett* and the short stories). His conclusion is that Cozzens is a writer of classical temperament and strongly intellectual disposition whose preference goes to the traditional forms of fiction.

A4 Michel, Pierre. *James Gould Cozzens*. Twayne United States Authors Series. New York: Twayne Publishers, forthcoming, biblio., index.

Considers Cozzens' fiction chronologically through *Morning Noon and Night* and devotes a full chapter each to the short stories and to Cozzens' "conservatism." Michel's concern is with the continuity and evolution of Cozzens' craft and themes throughout his whole work, each novel being assessed critically. Cozzens' best artistic achievement is *Guard of Honor*, which achieves "a remarkable fusion of form and content." *By Love Possessed* and *Morning Noon and Night* are less successful because of their inflated style, mannerisms, and overall shallowness.

A5 Mooney, Harry John, Jr. *James Gould Cozzens: Novelist of Intellect*. Critical Essays in Modern Literature. Pittsburgh: University of Pittsburgh Press, 1963. 186 pp.

Examines the eight novels from *S.S. San Pedro* to *By Love Possessed* from a thematic standpoint and concentrates, not on a critical assessment of Cozzens' fiction, but on his view of man and commitment to reason. There is a profound division in Cozzens' characters "between those hoping, in one way or another, for certainties, and those for whom the only certainty lies in the knowledge that certainties do not exist." According to Mooney, the movement from the first level of belief to the second constitutes the major theme of all of Cozzens' work. He devotes his last chapter to a balanced review of the main items in Cozzens criticism.

Criticism in books

B1 Adams, Richard P. "James Gould Cozzens: A Cultural Dilemma," in *Essays in Modern American Literature*, Richard E. Langford, ed. Stetson Studies in Humanities, No. 1. Deland, Fla.: Stetson University Press, 1963. pp. 103-111.

The only critic to argue that Cozzens' most pervasive theme is change, that "intellectually, he is convinced that change is universal, necessary, and inevitable; and [that] in this respect he belongs squarely in the romantic tradition of dynamic relativism or pragmatism." But acknowledges that Cozzens' style and imagery are ill-suited for such a theme and that he therefore remains "a romantic mind unable to divorce itself from a classic temperament."

B2 Allen, Walter. *Tradition and Dream. The English and American Novel from the Twenties to Our Time*. London: Phoenix House, 1964. pp. 185-187.

Brief and perceptive comments on *By Love Possessed*, *Guard of Honor*, *The Just and the Unjust*, and *Men and Brethren*. Cozzens is "pre-eminently the novelist of man in society . . . but the main emphasis is on society itself." Cozzens' awareness of the limits imposed on man's freedom to act "leads him to a deep conservatism." His chief deficiency is an absence of "poetry."

B3 Blackmur, Richard P. *The Expense of Greatness*. Gloucester, Mass.: Peter Smith, 1958. pp. 186-188.

Men and Brethren has excellent management "in the way of excitement, compactness, and the achieved air of momentum." The tone is set by a civilized, ironic sensibility; the theme is impressive: "what life does to a man who has already matured in a special way." But not enough attention is given to Cudlipp's feelings, and the main character falls short of being "eminent," and the novel, therefore, of being a great novel.

B4   Davies, Horton. *A Mirror of the Ministry in Modern Novels.* New York: Oxford University Press, 1959. pp. 153-164.

An excellent analysis of *Men and Brethren* as a ,,study . . . of the Protestant minister." Davies notes the variety, fullness, and accuracy of the clerical portraits the novel presents: "a profound understanding of the ministry as an exhausting, always interrupted, intelligent, and compassionate treating of mankind as the brethren of Christ." But the novel has one serious flaw : Cozzens seems unable to make poor or unprofessional people interesting. His lower-income-bracket characters are stereotypes, and religion hardly means more than decent morality for him.

B5   Eisinger, Chester E. "James Gould Cozzens: The Pennsylvania Voice of Aggressive Aristocracy," in his *Fiction of the Forties.* Chicago and London: University of Chicago Press, 1963. pp. 150-171.

An analysis of Cozzens' "conservatism" rather than of his art. Cozzens belongs to a dual tradition of the novel of manners and the aristocratic-conservative tradition. "Against the intellectual liberalism that survived into the forties, he posed a vigorous anti-intellectual conservatism; against the synthetic avantgardism of some of the new fiction of the decade, he posed the conservative, old-fashioned Jane Austen-George Eliot kind of novel." Cozzens is the bigoted, "aggressive white American Protestant" who feels that he is being relegated into a minority by the status revolution, and who turns for his ideology to

T. S. Eliot, Burke, Dewey, and the Stoics. Also notes that Cozzens "shares in the well-known American sex hostility and inhibition" and that, consequently, his women are not convincing as women. Concludes that Cozzens will never penetrate the reaches of great art "because art is dependent ultimately upon imagination and emotion," which he lacks.

B6   Fiedler, Leslie A. In *The Thirties. A Reconsideration in the Light of the American Political Tradition*, Morton J. Frisch and Martin Diamond, eds. De Kalb, Ill.: Northern Illinois University Press, 1968. pp. 60-62.
Interprets *Castaway* as an allegory portraying the end of "independent bourgeois enterprise" and "modern capitalism," and reads into it some of "the deep despair which really moved the Thirties" and which was able to move Cozzens "out of [his] sluggish iciness and abstraction."

B7   French, Warren. In *The Forties: Fiction, Poetry, Drama*, Warren French, ed. Deland, Fla.: Everett/Edwards, Inc., 1969. pp. 10-15.
Because of Cozzens' avoidance of emotion, his novels lack both color and depth. "Motivated by some kind of faith . . . in the necessity of maintaining some kind of 'life-force'," Cozzens is reluctant to commit himself, and this "lack of forthrightness" deprives *Guard of Honor* of vitality. His philosophy goes beyond conservatism; his passive acquiescence to the status quo is a "sophisticated form of despair." Finally, "Cozzens has learned to veil his distaste for the rest of mankind beneath a mask of sophisticated rationalism."

B8   Frohock, W. M. "Cozzens and His Critics: A Problem in Perspective," in his *Strangers to This Ground*. Dallas: Southern Methodist University Press, 1961. pp. 63-83.
Examines one critic in particular, Dwight Macdonald, who according to Frohock exaggerated his attack on the style of *By*

Love Possessed and who cannot understand Cozzens because he
does not belong to the same "culture." Frohock then goes on
to show that, though in *By Love Possessed* Cozzens does not leave
his reader much choice as to what his interpretation should be,
in this and his other novels he describes a way of life that is not
inconsistent with reality. Whether one likes or dislikes that
reality should not influence one's aesthetic judgment.

B9 Gardiner, Harold Charles, S.J. "Monument to Hollow
    Men," in his *In All Conscience. Reflections on Books and
    Culture*. Garden City, N.Y.: Hanover House, 1959.
    pp. 143-144.
    Reprint of D156.

B10 Guttmann, Allen. "James Gould Cozzens, Realist," in
    his *The Conservative Tradition in America*. New York:
    Oxford University Press, 1967. pp. 168-175.

    Guttmann gives synopses of six of Cozzens' novels and briefly
    explains their themes; he devotes most of his attention to *Men
    and Brethren, The Just and the Unjust, Guard of Honor*, and *By Love
    Possessed*, which best express Cozzens' philosophy and are good
    novels. Although he repeatedly calls Cozzens a "Conservative,"
    Guttmann fails to indicate exactly to what conservative tradition
    he belongs.

B11 Hart, James D. *The Oxford Companion to American
    Literature*. New York: Oxford University Press, 1965.
    pp. 190-191.

B12 Healey, Robert C. In *Fifty Years of the American Novel.
    A Christian Appraisal*, Harold C. Gardiner, ed. New
    York-London: Charles Scribner's Sons, 1951.
    pp. 268-269.

    A short and balanced appraisal of *Guard of Honor*: "The most
    solid and satisfying of all the novels which deal directly with

Americans in war [by] a conscientious artist who takes a broad, objective view and rejects specious sensational effects."

B13 Janowitz, Morris. *The Professional Soldier: A Social and Political Portrait*. Glencoe, Ill.: The Free Press of Glencoe, 1960. p. 5.

Guard of Honor "depicts intimate, interpersonal relations . . . rather than the organizational dilemmas of war-making."

B14 Kunitz, Stanley J. and Howard Haycraft, eds. *Twentieth Century Authors*. New York: H. W. Wilson Co., 1942. pp. 323-324.

Quotes Cozzens on biographical data.

B15 Kunitz, Stanley J. and Vineta Colby, eds. *Twentieth Century Authors, First Supplement*. New York: H. W. Wilson Co., 1955. p. 241.

B16 Lewis, R. W. "The Conflicts of Reality: Cozzens' *The Last Adam*," in *Seven Contemporary Authors*, Thomas Whitbread, ed. Austin and London: University of Texas Press, 1966. pp. 1-22.

A thorough and excellent analysis of the themes and technique of *The Last Adam* as a "skillfully *patterned* novel" which "foreshadows many of [the] later themes and techniques." First notes that Cozzens belongs to the tradition of realism and of the novel (as opposed to the romance) and that he is mainly concerned with man in society. Lewis bases his analysis on the "ambiguities, dilemmas, and tensions" which form *The Last Adam*'s large "thematic pattern of conflicts." In his opinion, "Cozzens is artful in the interweaving of his episodes into the single pattern that through character, image, symbol, and theme as well as action demonstrates the complex, conflicting nature of Cozzens' vision of reality."

B17 Magill, Frank N. and Dayton Kohler, eds. *Masterplots: Cyclopedia of World Authors*. New York: Salem Press, 1958, 2 vols. Vol. 1, 251-252.

B18 Maxwell, D. E. S. *American Fiction: The Intellectual Background*. London: Routledge and Kegan Paul; New York: Columbia University Press, 1963. pp. 278-287.

Briefly examines *Castaway*, *The Just and the Unjust*, and *Guard of Honor*. Points to *Castaway*'s similarities and dissimilarities with Poe's stories, and emphasizes the political issues which the latter two novels dramatize. Cozzens' subject is "the alternations of inflexibility and pliableness by which the social order retains its equilibrium." Concludes with a few short remarks on the "flexibility of [Cozzens'] style, the intricacies of his formal prose alleviated by his ear for the living idiom, the familiar making lively contact with the cultivated."

B19 Miller, Wayne Charles. *An Armed America: Its Face in Fiction*. New York: New York University Press; London: University of London Press, 1970. pp. 188-204.

Cozzens is a "detached and perceptive observer." Miller bases his discussion of *Guard of Honor* on a systematic analysis of the characters as they relate to one another in the complex organism of the base. He concludes that Cozzens "makes no moral judgment concerning the professional versus the citizen-soldier, . . . does not regard warfare as immoral, . . . does not view the military élite as self-consciously pursuing power. He most closely resembles those other World War II novelists who accepted warfare as a brutal but normal human experience."

B20 Millgate, Michael. *American Social Fiction: James to Cozzens*. Edinburgh and London: Oliver and Boyd; New York: Barnes and Noble, 1964. pp. 181-194.

Like John Brooks, Cozzens is seized with the passion to record, but he is "more impressive and more politically engaged." In *The Last Adam, Men and Brethren*, and *The Just and the Unjust*, Cozzens "points out the sad inadequacies of conventional moral values and professional ethics when confronted with the often shocking demands of actual living." In *Guard of Honor*, he displays "considerable technical skill in the intricate interweaving of characters, incidents, and subplots." We accept the novel's "wisdom" because it is stated as simple truth. This is not true of *By Love Possessed*, whose "wisdom" is pretentious and whose style is ponderous and verbose. Cozzens "has less assurance in presenting intimate personal relationships than in analysing the fine shadings of hierarchical relationships. Passion seems to carry a negative connotation in [his] moral world. [He] often strikes us as too dispassionate, too limited in his sympathies, too unresponsive to 'the promises of life'."

B21 Mizener, Arthur. "The Novel and Nature in the Twentieth Century: Anthony Powell and James Gould Cozzens," in his *The Sense of Life in the Modern Novel*. Boston: Houghton Mifflin Co., 1964. pp. 79-103. Also, pp. 136-137.

More about Powell than about Cozzens. Notes the similarities and the contrasts between the two: they had to wait a long time for recognition, and "both recognize that men can express their natures at all only by means of a guard of honor or some other conventional form of behavior, firmly established in their society. Both are therefore fascinated by the elaborate rituals of society." Cozzens in particular "is fascinated by the persistence with which [men] assert their egos in an endless and unsuccessful attempt to control these rituals and dominate their societies." Cozzens distinguishes himself from Powell in his belief that "social patterns are almost natural forces of a violent and uncontrollable sort." His characters, who foresee and accept their inevitable confounding without ceasing to struggle, are, in the end, "far lonelier people than Powell's characters, for what they are is never in any important way reflected by what they succeed in doing."

B22 Mizener, Arthur. "James Gould Cozzens: *Guard of Honor*," in his *Twelve Great American Novels*. New York: New American Library, 1967. pp. 160-176.

Guard of Honor is a "full-scale realistic novel . . . unusual both in substance and in form." Mizener discusses Cozzens' background and critical reception. He underlines Cozzens' realism, objectivity, and anti-romanticism. His main theme is "what the problem of time and mortality is for the man who finds outer reality the significant one and is convinced that freedom is the recognition of necessity." Cozzens' novels have an old-fashioned subtlety and "beautiful, intricate pattern[s]." Reprint of C45.

B23 Noble, David W. *The Eternal Adam and the New World Garden. The Central Myth in the American Novel Since 1830*. New York: George Braziller, 1968. pp. 186-193.

Boorstin's theory of American history has found its popular expression in *By Love Possessed:* if European institutions and traditions have always been the foundation of social reality in America, the crossing of the Atlantic has just as often given them a pragmatic twist (abstract reasoning became practical education, ideology became political realism, etc.). Arthur Winner "is chosen by Cozzens to carry the burden of initiating Americans into the reality of existence, to demonstrate the necessity of conducting oneself as a Man of Reason and accepting the status quo."

B24 Nyren, Dorothy, ed. *A Library of Literary Criticism. Modern American Literature*. New York: Frederick Ungar, 1960. pp. 111-115.

Cites excerpts from fifteen important reviews or articles on
Cozzens.

B25 Prescott, Orville. *In My Opinion*. Indianapolis-New
York: Bobbs-Merrill Co., 1952. pp. 182-191.

Cozzens is one of the most distinguished living American writers
who gives "remarkably penetrating interpretations of the general
community life." His fiction has "an authentic ring of truth, . . .
[a] firm and quiet eloquence." One reservation: "his technical
facility, irony, wit and cruelly analytic characterizations [seem]
the products of a cold-blooded craftsmanship immune to feeling."
The appeal of Cozzens' fiction is primarily to the mind and it
leaves the reader emotionally uninvolved, though there are
echoes of "true compassion and a sort of stoic wisdom" in *The
Just and the Unjust* and *Guard of Honor*.

B26 Rothe, Anna, ed. *Current Biography*. New York: H. W.
Wilson Co., 1950. pp. 125-127.

B27 Stuckey, W. J. *The Pulitzer Prize Novels; A Critical
Backward Look*. Norman: University of Oklahoma
Press, 1966. pp. 143-151.

Cozzens' main interest lies in the public and private relationships
of his characters and in the social, moral, and philosophical
implications of these relationships. His "philosophy" (the art of
the possible) is conservative insofar as he is more or less
satisfied with the way things are.

B28 Walcutt, Charles Child. *Man's Changing Mask: Modes
and Methods of Characterization in Fiction*. Minneapolis:
University of Minnesota Press, 1966. pp. 280-286.

Walcutt's thesis is that some novelists base their novels on ideas
which "may inspire very successful characterizations when they
are expressed through significant actions." The "idea" behind
By Love Possessed is a belief in a "code of reason," a knowledge

of the human condition, and a final conviction that "expediency prevail[s] over honor." The rhythms of Arthur Winner's thought, so often condemned as involuted and verbose, reflect the rhythms of the town and of life; "the action is tremendously exciting, the style is compelling, the theme is profoundly rooted in the study of man in society."

B29 Waldmeir, Joseph J. *American Novels of the Second World War*. Studies in American Literature, No. 20. The Hague-Paris: Mouton, 1969. pp. 130-137.

Waldmeir focusses on the racial issue in *Guard of Honor*, which is "a straightforward defense of the status quo, a clear, unmistakable attack on intellectual liberalism, and a strong argument for middle-of-the-road white supremacy." Waldmeir concludes that "it might be argued . . . that Wouk and Cozzens are in reality little more than ideological neo-Fascists."

B30 Warfel, Harry R. *American Novelists of Today*. New York: American Book Co., 1951. p. 103.

Criticism in periodicals

C1   Albrecht, W. P. "War and Fraternity: A Study of Some Recent American War Novels," *New Mexico Quarterly Review*, 21, No. 4 (Winter 1951), 461-474 (Cozzens, 469, 472).

C2   Boulger, James D. "Puritan Allegory in Four Modern Novels," *Thought*, 44, No. 174 (Autumn 1969), 413-432.

Examines O'Connor's *The Last Hurrah*, Ellison's *Invisible Man*, Bellow's *Herzog*, and Cozzens' *By Love Possessed*, and perceives in the four novels "a similar allegorical religious pattern." Bases his argument on the Puritan-Calvinist theology whose pattern is one of a journey leading from Election to Vocation and finally to Sanctification. "What all this adds up to is an abbreviated and attenuated version of the common Christian sense of life as a journey and an imitation of Christ." Boulger interprets Arthur Winner's story along such lines, pointing out however that the specifically theological framework is deliberately avoided by Cozzens. Winner "undergoes three trials of Vocation as means of determining the significance of his Election by birth and right to highest status." The basic allegory of the journey to glorification is fulfilled in the final section of the novel.

C3   Bracher, Frederick. "James Gould Cozzens: Humanist," *Critique*, 1, No. 3 (Winter 1958), 10-29.

Cozzens' most obvious characteristic is his deliberate avoidance of literary fashion. His main theme is that proper study is the condition of man, and he prefers to choose his "admirable" characters from among the educated professional and executive class (and hence has little sympathy for the young and those outside that class). His philosophy, which may be called stoic, is that one must work within the limits of the possible, which implies an "acceptance of fallible humanity [and a] rueful resignation to the unsatisfactory state of things in general." Cozzens expresses a preference for established institutions and traditions, for the law, for small isolated communities that provide their members with a sense of belonging; he consistently understates the value of romantic love and stresses the destructive power of the amative appetite. Bracher implies that he lacks a sense of social vision, but stresses his "concern for form and craftsmanship" and notes his clever use of the three unities. The characters are convincing; Bracher notes the "subtlety of the analysis [and] the articulate richness of its expression"; the style, which is generally "rich, sonorous and masculine, . . . enriched by allusions and literary echoes," sometimes degenerates into a "Chinese puzzle." Finally he states that "irony pervades the novels," but does not elaborate.

C4 Bracher, Frederick. "Of Youth and Age: James Gould Cozzens," *Pacific Spectator*, 5, No. 1 (Winter 1951), 48-62.

One of the pioneering articles. Bracher prefers to dwell on Cozzens' qualities rather than on his limitations. He analyzes the "four major novels so far": *The Last Adam*, *Men and Brethren*, *The Just and the Unjust*, and *Guard of Honor*. "Cozzens is a philosophic novelist in the same sense that George Eliot is: he has a passion for analyzing and explaining what he observes." Then he explains Cozzens' "philosophy": "an almost complacent acceptance of inequalities in human kind," and a belief in an unillusioned sense of realism. "The Cozzens heroes are not heroic in any ideal sense. Middle-aged and unromantic, they are admirable because they have accepted the obligations of maturity." No discussion of the formal aspects of the novels.

C5   Coxe, Louis O. "A High Place," *Critique*, 1, No. 3
      (Winter 1958), 48-51.

With each new novel, Cozzens' style "develops, becomes
marvellously various and tough, the vocabulary grows in
subtlety and allusiveness, the syntax increases in packed
suppleness." As a result, *By Love Possessed* is "a novel of masterly
ironic incident, great complexity, and high style." But it lacks a
central action and its protagonist lacks features and form.
Moreover, Cozzens intrudes a little too blatantly into his
characters' opinions and views.

C6   Coxe, Louis O. "The Complex World of James Gould
      Cozzens," *American Literature*, 27, No. 2 (May 1955),
      157-171.

Cozzens examines "the double vision of modern man, the central
paradox of action and contemplation, of understanding and
conduct, of the ironic view and the heroic efficacy, . . . initiation
into the world of complexity, . . . moral obliquity, the question
of salvation by grace or by works, or by neither, the problem
of power and its necessity." Taking the position that life is a
tragic affair, Cozzens is the legitimate heir of Hawthorne,
Melville and perhaps Poe. Coxe notes that Cozzens is unique in
the use of a "ratiocinative technique superimposed on a dramatic,
almost melodramatic, subject matter, and one of the excitements
of the best work derives from the tension vibrating between these
seeming irreconcilabilities." He praises his style, which is
muscular, virile, and has strong affinities to seventeenth-century
prose and displays a strong command of "a range of idiom,
allusion, cadence, rhetorical radiation and vocabulary."

C7   DeMott, Benjamin. "Cozzens and Others," *Hudson
      Review*, 10, No. 4 (Winter 1957-58), 620-626.

As a rule Cozzens is more interested in professions than in living
people. But *By Love Possessed* "deserves praise as a local success
at the difficult task of elevating contemporary experience to the

point at which it becomes interesting; it stands as a rare
opportunity . . . for the reader to lift himself briefly out of the
sloughs of self-contempt into which the next new American
novel he confronts will undoubtedly be determined to plunge
him."

C8   Duggan, Francis X. "Facts and All Man's Fiction,"
      Thought, 33, No. 131 (Winter 1958-59), 604-616.

Argues that from *Confusion* to *By Love Possessed* Cozzens has
devoted his energy to working out a single view of life: "How
shall man meet the torrent of circumstances ?" This question
is illustrated in all of Cozzens' novels by a conflict of will
against circumstances in which his heroes merely try to contain
the disorder of the world. Duggan notes that there is in Cozzens
an increasing narrowness of range, and concludes that he "must
either find some new direction for his art or fall into exhausting
repetitions of the same old thing." In addition, Cozzens'
judgment on life "has so possessed the artist [in *By Love
Possessed*] that it threatens the vitality and integrity of his work."
As for the style, from "spare and swift" in a novel like *S.S. San
Pedro*, it becomes "perverse" in the later prose.

C9   Eisinger, Chester E. "The American War Novel: An
      Affirming Flame," *Pacific Spectator*, 9, No 3 (Summer
      1955), 272-287.

Finds that there are many similarities between Dewey's and
Cozzens' philosophies; Cozzens forges a realism that recognizes
the dynamism of society but, contrary to Dewey, perversely
defends the status quo.

C10   Eisinger, Chester E. "The Voice of Aggressive
      Aristocracy," *Midway*, No. 18, Spring 1964, pp. 100-
      128.

Reprint of B5.

C11 Fergusson, Francis. "Three Novels," *Perspectives USA*, No. 6, Winter 1954, pp. 30-44.

Examines *Guard of Honor* together with R. P. Warren's *All the King's Men* and Lionel Trilling's *The Middle of the Journey*. Admits that, in its picture of a large aggregation of lives, *Guard of Honor* "is organized with superb intelligence." Colonel Ross is a moralizer and "without his moralizing the novel would have no shape at all"; his philosophy is adequate to the Air Base but "inadequate to the war." *Guard of Honor* is close to "the best journalism."

C12 Finn, James. "Cozzens Dispossessed," *Commonweal*, 68 (April 4, 1958), 11-13.

Cozzens' main theme is the clash between a recognizable objective code and responsible, individual decision; his technique is that of the nineteenth-century novelist, minus the originality and audacity. But in *By Love Possessed* Cozzens departs from his former manner in two ways: he uses a prose "that is, for long stretches, singularly costive," and his handling of some of his characters is so clumsy that it is damaging to them. Finn's conclusion: Cozzens' mind "is, finally, unoriginal, unimaginative, uninteresting."

C13 Fowler, Alastair. "Isolation and Its Discontents," *Twentieth Century Literature*, 6, No. 2 (July 1960), 51-64.

A Freudian interpretation that stresses the symbolic character of *Castaway*. Fowler first argues that Lecky's "isolation is a predicament of the whole man, a mysterious, even supernatural isolation: complete, profound, and enduring" that is symbolic of all of mankind's predicament. He then explains *Castaway* along two concomitant lines: "no better image than the store could have been found for the psychosis within which capitalist society is compulsively imprisoned"; and Cozzens "explores as enduring springs of action, and subjects man's frailty to the same steadfast appraisal, as Freud, whose insights . . . he used. *Castaway* followed *Civilization and Its Discontents* in deriving guilt from original aggression."

C14 Frederick, John T. "Fiction of the Second World War," *College English*, 17, No. 4 (January 1956), 197-204.

Because of its complex pattern, with a large and crowded canvas, *Guard of Honor* "is an intellectual achievement of a high order." Another quality of Cozzens is that "he dramatizes social problems only to the one end of fiction, the illumination of Man through men."

C15 Frederick, John T. "Love by Adverse Possession: The Case of Mr. Cozzens," *College English*, 19, No. 7 (April 1958), 313-316.

Though an admirer of *The Just and the Unjust* and *Guard of Honor*, Frederick dismisses *By Love Possessed* as an inferior novel. It is "digressive, flaccid in structure, ultimately dull," its style too often ponderous. As a treatise on love, it is inadequate because, by putting excessive emphasis on only one part of it, Cozzens is "false to the general truth of human experience." Finally, Cozzens is particularly unfair in his treatment of Catholicism.

C16 Frost, William. "Cozzens: Some Reservations about *By Love Possessed*," *College English*, 19, No. 7 (April 1958), 317-318.

Objects to *By Love Possessed*'s characterizations ("puppets"), style ("over-rhetorical"), dialogue ("literary"), point of view ("crude and oversimple"), and setting (Brocton is a mere abstraction).

C17 Garrett, George. "*By Love Possessed:* The Pattern and the Hero," *Critique*, 1, No. 3 (Winter 1958), 41-47.

By Love Possessed "offers the most thorough exploitation of the pattern of ordered experience" which identifies a Cozzens novel.

Like all the "mature" novels, it immerses itself in the discipline
of a profession and is shaped by a single center of consciousness;
other elements of importance are the past, the small town, and
the compression of time. Cozzens' language, "though rich, is
superficially simple, direct and transparent"; though discursive,
often in an after-the-fact, expository manner, "it remains a marvel
of lucidity."

C18 Geismar, Maxwell. "By Cozzens Possessed," *Critique*,
1, No. 3 (Winter 1958), 51-53. Reprinted in his
American Moderns. From Rebellion to Conformity. New
York: Hill and Wang, 1958. pp. 145-150.

Argues that Cozzens lacks "some charge of primary emotion
which might give his work more color" and that his fiction
lacks the sense of the ordinary experiences of living.

C19 Hamblen, Abigail Ann. "The Paradox of James Gould
Cozzens," *Western Humanities Review*, 19, No. 4
(Autumn 1965), 355-361.

Discerns in Cozzens an acute consciousness of man's inequality
(racial, economic, social, intellectual) and an apprehension of the
possibility of innate evil, but also a belief in love and in
"brotherliness," all of which define his "philosophy of
acceptance."

C20 Harding, D. W. "Earlier Cozzens," *Spectator*, 6809
(December 26, 1958), 923.

Brief comments on the novels from *S.S. San Pedro* to *Guard of
Honor*. Emphasizes Cozzens' perfectionism in form, but Harding
is mistaken when he states that the English edition of *Guard of
Honor* contains "fairly numerous" revisions.

C21 Hermann, John. "Cozzens and a Critic," *College English*,
19, No. 7 (April 1958), 316-317.

A rebuttal of Lydenberg's "Cozzens and the Critics" [see C36].
By Love Possessed is an inferior novel because Cozzens consistently
minimizes opponents for the glory of his hero ("Sir Arthur")
and loses control of his style.

C22 Hicks, Granville. "The Case for Cozzens," *Saturday
Review*, 42, No. 32 (August 8, 1959), 12.

In the course of his review of Bracher's book [see A1] ("an
effort to contribute to the understanding of Cozzens rather than
to blow up his reputation"), Hicks makes a balanced judgment
of Cozzens' work: "He has shown a greater capacity for growth
than the majority of his contemporaries. He clings tenaciously to
his own point of view, and it yields him a vision of human
experience that the reader has to respect even when he doesn't
like it."

C23 Hicks, Granville. "The Reputation of James Gould
Cozzens," *English Journal*, 39, No. 1 (January 1950),
1-7. Also in *College English*, 11, No. 4 (January 1950),
177-183.

One of the first perceptive articles. Stresses Cozzens' "authority,"
objectivity, "passionate detachment," avoidance of
pretentiousness, never fuzzy imagery, ear for many varieties of
speech, authentic dialogue, and skill in developing a complex
but clear structure. Notes that Cozzens "stands completely
outside the tradition of revolt," and alludes to, but does not
define, his conservatism. Regrets that Cozzens' novels lack some
of the "vitality that is the essence of imaginative literature."

C24 Hinchliffe, Arnold P. "The End of a Dream?" *Studi
Americani*, 5 (1959), 315-323.

Hinchliffe's thesis is that "the central moral crisis is Arthur
Winner's, and it is his innocence that is exploited, denied and
re-affirmed in new terms." Like Nelson Algren in *Never Come
Morning* and Jack Kerouac in *On the Road*, Cozzens, in *By Love*

Possessed, "examine[s] the dream in the three stages of man, and offer[s], ultimately, only death, disillusionment or duplicity as alternatives for living."

C25 Hyman, Stanley E. "James Gould Cozzens and the Art of the Possible," *New Mexico Quarterly*, 19, No. 4 (Winter 1949), 476-498.

Holds *Castaway* as Cozzens' "most successful work" ("The book's range of meaning is very great, and its allegory translates readily into half-a-dozen frames of reference"). The main themes of the novels are the concept of "earned" morality, the radical imperfectibility of man, power and authority, chance and luck, the impulse to self-hurt or self-destruction, and the passage of time. Because of its realism and "heavily researched quality," Cozzens' fiction belongs to the Balzac-Zola tradition. Cozzens' least attractive feature is that he is "the novelist of the American White Protestant middle class," with all its stock prejudices and sexual frustrations and dissatisfactions. Cozzens' qualities are "his enormously representative quality and his uncompromising honesty, . . . his constantly augmented scope," his perfect grasp of the scenic. His shortcomings are his tendencies to substitute melodrama for drama or "to sprawl, and thus lack tension and excitement."

C26 Hyman, Stanley E. "My Favorite Forgotten Book," *Tomorrow*, 7 (May 1947), 58-59.

Because of its technique of meticulous and detailed realism, *Castaway* is a *tour de force*; it is written with "a sense of real style. . . . It shares Kafka's method of the 'unmotivated scene'." Its meaning: "Just as the fable of a castaway building an idyllic private empire expresses the burgeoning social optimism of Defoe's class and century, so this latter-day fable of a castaway . . . seems to express the hopeless pessimism of the same class in our day. It is . . . a social allegory: of the corruption of human relations by property relations; of freedom and

personality gained in our society only through murder, . . . or
war itself. . . . It is, equally, a psychoanalytic fable of the
repression of Id by Ego and the consequent punishment by
Super-Ego; or a religious fable of sin and expiation; or even an
Evolutionary fable of the development of man." Whatever its
meaning, "it is in the tradition of the American supernatural
story, the moral allegories of Hawthorne and Henry James":
a projection of the evil heart of man.

C27 Janeway, Elizabeth. "Guardian of Middle-Class
Honor," *New York Times Book Review*, August 9, 1959,
pp. 1, 18.

A review of Bracher's book [see A1]. Miss Janeway makes some
comments on Cozzens: he can write good dialogue (interestingly
enough, "often . . . his best dialogue is given to the characters
who are farthest from his own point of view"), but his style can
be clumsy. He does not see society as static and immutable, but
as "fragile, constantly challenged, and supporting itself only by
almost superhuman efforts." His heroes have serious limitations:
they never (nor does Cozzens) explore the question "What is
power and why do we want it ?"; they never wonder whether
something other than the status quo would be more satisfactory;
finally, they lack a minimum of passion that would make them
a little more human.

C28 Lamport, Felicia. "By Henry James Cozened: A
Parody," *Audience*, 5, No. 3 (Summer 1958), 30-35.
A parody of *By Love Possessed*.

C29 Leonard, Frank G. "Cozzens without Sex; Steinbeck
without Sin," *Antioch Review*, 18, No. 2 (Summer 1958),
209-218.

Discusses the *Reader's Digest* condensation of *By Love Possessed*
and John Steinbeck's *East of Eden*, and points to the various
"improvements," moral and stylistic, as significant in a
definition of mass culture.

C30 Levenson, J. C. "Prudence and Perdition," *Critique*, 1, No. 3 (Winter 1958), 53-54.

The Son of Perdition, a minor *Nostromo*, "limited in scale and realistic in tone," is one of Cozzens' best novels. In his later work, Cozzens makes prudence his constant theme: "what he leaves out is the foolishness which may be wisdom."

C31 Long, Richard A. "The Image of Man in James Gould Cozzens," *CLA Journal*, 10, No. 4 (June 1967), 299-307.

Long says nothing new until his last paragraph, where he states that Cozzens' view of man is artistically faulty, an assertion that would have been interesting if he had been able to document it.

C32 Loomis, Edward W. "A Note on Cozzens," *Spectrum*, 4, No. 2 (Spring-Summer 1960), 96-98.

Considers *Men and Brethren*, *Guard of Honor*, and *By Love Possessed*. Loomis' argument is twofold: the pattern of Cozzens' novels is defective because "the collocation of trying events within a short period of time is necessarily a fortuitous occurrence," the "given" of these novels is merely a piece of bad luck, and "the events composing the hero's test are for the most part not significantly related to one another."

C33 Ludwig, Richard M. "A Reading of the James Gould Cozzens Manuscripts," *Princeton University Library Chronicle*, 19, No. 1 (Autumn 1957), 1-14. Reprinted under title "The Cozzens Papers" in *Princeton Alumni Weekly*, 58 (May 30, 1958), 7-9, 13.

A few comments on some of the novels, especially *Guard of Honor* and *By Love Possessed* ("the enormous scope, the narrative power, the explorations of moral responsibility"). Then a description of the Cozzens papers deposited at the Princeton University Library in 1957. Particularly valuable for several quotations from Cozzens' letters which reveal his deep and unchanging concern with his craft and philosophy and for samples of the many revisions which *By Love Possessed* underwent. A checklist of Cozzens' novels and stories up to 1957 (only in the *Princeton University Library Chronicle*).

C34 Ludwig, Richard M. "James Gould Cozzens: A Review of Research and Criticism," *Texas Studies in Literature and Language*, 1, No. 1 (Spring 1959), 123-136.

Four sections include bibliography and manuscripts, editions and reprints, biography and criticism. This latter section is particularly valuable for a survey of the ups and downs of Cozzens criticism from Hyman's essay [see C26] to the special issue of *Critique* (1958).

C35 Lydenberg, John. "Cozzens and the Conservatives," *Critique*, 1, No. 3 (Winter 1958), 3-9.

The first attempt to define Cozzens' "conservatism." Finds similarities between Cozzens' "philosophy" and neo-conservatism: a distrust of the liberal tradition, pessimism about human nature, an awareness of the natural inequalities of men, and an acceptance of the leadership of an established, cultured aristocracy. Cozzens' ethics is an ethic of responsibility, "responsibility to the well-tested, traditional virtues of a rational, moral society." He is a throwback to the eighteenth century, but strictly to the "conservative, realistic wing of eighteenth century thought that rejected the revolutionary or Jeffersonian ardors." Lydenberg gives three reasons why Cozzens is not popular, even among his fellow conservatives: he is no prophet; his respect for the conservative virtues does not rest on the rock of religion; preferring old families, whose sense of proprieties is instinctive, he shuns the sentimentality that accompanies middle-class respectability.

C36 Lydenberg, John. "Cozzens and the Critics," *College English*, 19, No. 3 (December 1957), 99-104.

Gives the following reasons for the relative neglect of Cozzens by critics until *By Love Possessed*, at least: his self-imposed seclusion; the fact that he falls into none of the convenient patterns the critics are accustomed to finding; the fact that he merely records normal life in the tradition of nineteenth-century moral realism; his pessimistic view of the world; his books present no difficult problem of interpretation, no "deeper" meanings, no "ultimate" significances. [See C21]

C37 Lydenberg, John. "Cozzens' Man of Responsibility," *Shenandoah*, 10 (Winter 1959), 11-18.

The first consistent definition of Cozzens' "conservatism." After *The Last Adam*, Cozzens' heroes are exclusively pillars of their society, upholders of order, exemplars of the gentle, the genteel, the good, men of responsibility for whom active works are the way to salvation. With Jefferson, Cozzens believes that a democracy must be led by the aristocracy of virtue and talents; with John Adams, that this natural aristocracy will most often coincide with the aristocracy of birth and wealth. But these aristocrats are not in the least concerned with the fate of their society, nor with any of the themes that infuse contemporary fiction; they are merely dedicated to the preservation of order, i.e. the status quo.

C38 Marx, Leo. "Controversy," *American Scholar*, 27, No. 2 (Spring 1958), 228-229.

In answer to C70. Disagrees with Ward's implication that Cozzens' vogue is a measure of the American people's new maturity; Marx rather sees in it something "akin to the apathy and moral resignation" of the Eisenhower era. Cozzens' quietism "seems to sanction a regression, a dangerous withdrawal from the realities of historical change."

C39 Marysková, Květa. "Cesty do hlubin Americké literatury," *Časopis pro moderní filologii*, 44, 36-44.

In *By Love Possessed*, "an elaborate technique is applied to trifles, petty problems and anomalous characters. The viewpoint of Cozzens, interwoven in the structure of the novel, is that evil, when encountered is to be accepted and not combatted, that it is futile to attempt to change inherited conditions. *By Love Possessed* is a novel of conformism and its acclaim was similarly not justified on literary grounds" (quoted from summary).

C40 Mazzara, Richard A. " 'Misère et grandeur de l'homme': Pascal's *Pensées* and Cozzens' *By Love Possessed*," *Ball State Teachers College Forum*, 5, No. 1 (1964), 17-20.

A rather unconvincing comparison between the *Pensées* and *By Love Possessed* ; if these two writers indeed "lead the reader rigorously to accept one conclusion, to follow a more human and sane middle path between the extremes of man's *grandeur* and his *misère*," then many writers must be alike. Certainly there are more dissimilarities than similarities between Cozzens and Pascal. The comparison between Arthur Winner's life and Pascal's is even less convincing.

C41 Meriwether, James B. "A James Gould Cozzens Checklist," *Critique*, 1, No. 3 (Winter 1958), 57-63.

The first Cozzens checklist. It was for a long time the only one of value.

C42 Meriwether, James B. "The English Editions of James Gould Cozzens," *Studies in Bibliography*, 15 (1962), 207-217.

Discusses revisions made in the English or American editions of *Michael Scarlett*, *Castaway*, and *S.S. San Pedro*. The English text of *Michael Scarlett* underwent minor revisions; in the case of

Castaway, the American text is clearly the better; Meriwether admits that his evidence as to which of the various texts of *S.S. San Pedro* is definitive is inconclusive and that much work remains to be done.

C43 Michel, Pierre. "A Note on James Gould Cozzens," *Revue des Langues Vivantes*, 26, No. 3 (1960), 192-209.

A discussion of the main themes in *The Last Adam*, *Ask Me Tomorrow*, *Men and Brethren*, *The Just and the Unjust*, *Guard of Honor*, and *By Love Possessed*.

C44 Millgate, Michael. "The Judgements of James Gould Cozzens," *Critical Quarterly*, 4, No. 1 (Spring 1962), 87-91.

A balanced assessment of *S.S. San Pedro*, *Men and Brethren*, *Guard of Honor*, and *By Love Possessed* prompted by the critical excesses to which Millgate refers briefly. Emphasizes Cozzens' "deliberate unromanticism," his philosophy (the sad inadequacy of conventional moral values and professional ethics), his knowledge of man, his "considerable technical skill in the intricate interweaving of characters, incidents, and sub-plots," but also the verbosity, ponderousness, and pretentious style of *By Love Possessed* and Cozzens' inability to present "intimate personal relationships." Millgate concludes that Cozzens "is the equal of all but the greatest of modern American writers."

C45 Mizener, Arthur. "The Undistorting Mirror," *Kenyon Review*, 28, No. 5 (1966), 595-611.

See B22.

C46 Mohrt, Michel. Preface to *Par l'Amour Possédé*, Marie Tadié trans. Paris: Albin Michel, 1960. pp. IX-XIV.

Views *By Love Possessed* as a document illustrating that "Amérique devenue insolite, . . . l'Amérique *Tory*, fière de sa tradition puritaine, de sa victoire sur le Sud" in which Cozzens holds one of the last isolationist bastions. The sociology of the novel is "reactionary"; one must see in Cozzens' conservatism "l'expression d'une mauvaise humeur, bien plus qu'une philosophie cohérente." But if a philosophy still is to be extracted from the novel, then it is a stoic acceptance of the human condition.

C47 *Newsweek*, 51, No. 17 (April 28, 1958), 98-99. "A Gadfly Stings Cozzens . . . For Best-Selling 'Possessed'."

On the background of the Cozzens-Macdonald quarrel following Macdonald's review in *Commentary* [see D168].

C48 *New York Times*, November 20, 1936, p. 21.

Announcement of the O. Henry Memorial Award (1936) for the best short story ("Total Stranger").

C49 *New York Times*, May 3, 1949, p. 22.

Short notice on occasion of the 1949 Pulitzer Prize (*Guard of Honor*).

C50 *New York Times*, June 20, 1952, p. 18.

Announcement of award of Honorary Doctor of Letters degree to Cozzens by Harvard.

C51 *New York Times*, September 3, 1968, p. 26.

Announcement of donation of typescript of *Morning Noon and Night* to the Princeton University Library.

C52 Ober, William B. *Carleton Miscellany*, 4, No. 4 (Fall 1963), 104-106.

The Last Adam is "a well realized piece of prose fiction. It is a valid example of the naturalistic-realistic school": the characters are plausible, their dialogue is recorded with a good ear. But the scope of the novel is narrow; it deals with ordinary people in a ordinary way and, therefore, is not very exciting.

C53 Parrish, James A., Jr. "James Gould Cozzens Fights a
War," *Arizona Quarterly*, 18, No. 4 (Winter 1962),
335-340.
Reveals some information about Cozzens' service in the Armed
Forces during World War II based on interviews of officers who
worked with him. Confirms Cozzens' "appetite for knowledge,
his moral realism, his extreme care in producing the enveloping
action, and his ability to create powerful scenes and significant
characters from ordinary experience."

C54 Pietro, Louis A. "La polemica en torno a James Gould
Cozzens," *Sur*, 256 (January-February 1959), 89-97.

C55 Powers, Richard H. "Praise the Mighty: Cozzens and
the Critics," *Southwest Review*, 43, No. 3 (Summer 1958),
263-270.
Argues that Cozzens "has truckled to the popular fancy which
the worst segment of upper-middle-class America has about
itself." The book is a political tract full of sentimental, class and
racial prejudices. Cozzens understands neither love nor sex.

C56 Prescott, Orville. *New York Times*, August 5, 1959,
p. 25.
Review of Bracher's book [see A1]. *By Love Possessed* "is one of
the finest American novels of recent years," written by a
novelist who has produced "far more accurate and significant
fictional interpretations of contemporary American life" than
other novelists like Faulkner or Hemingway.

C57 *Publishers' Weekly*, 189, No. 17 (April 25, 1966), 124.

C58 Rees, David. "Ministers of Fate," *Spectator*, 7143
(May 21, 1965), 666.
On Cozzens' novels from *S.S. San Pedro* on rather than on
Children and Others only, in which Rees discerns "a display of

Cozzens' analytic talents without the detail and the complexity of the situations he had made his own." Cozzens is not concerned with the potentialities of man–which present-day literature, essentially romantic, mainly is–but with his limitations. In the novels, "the underlying themes of man in society, the limits of action, and the curious, often irrational way in which institutional decisions evolve are controlled by two technical devices which remain broadly unaltered: the unities are usually preserved and, secondly, Cozzens's extremely detailed, allusive descriptive style means that we see his characters, and not only his leading characters, in almost Joycean depth. . . . The attitude that informs his work is not the conservative, but the classical."

C59 Rideout, Walter B. "James Gould Cozzens," *Critique*, 1, No. 3 (Winter 1958), 55-56.

The trouble with Cozzens is that his personal attitudes consciously or unconsciously limit his artistic intelligence; he suffers from prejudices and injects them into his fiction.

C60 *Scholastic*, 27, No. 14 (January 11, 1936), 6.

Anonymous biographical sketch.

C61 Scholes, Robert E. "The Commitment of James Gould Cozzens," *Arizona Quarterly*, 16, No. 2 (Summer 1960), 129-144.

An interesting study of the evolution of Cozzens' themes from the earlier novels to *By Love Possessed*. "Sensibility and emotional commitment" are present in the earlier novels "to the point of mawkishness perhaps"; in the later works, they are not absent but merely controlled. Scholes stresses the castigation and chastising of youth in much of Cozzens' body of fiction and his preoccupation with "men who do something" in the mature novels, which are all dominated by a professional ethic: the parable of the talents. He points to the main difference between

By Love Possessed and earlier works: "The problem of what to *do*, how to employ one's talent, which was so important in *Men and Brethren* and *The Just and the Unjust* is supplanted here by the transcendental problem of how to endure."

C62 Straumann, Heinrich. "The Quarrel about Cozzens or the Vagaries of Book Reviewing," *English Studies*, 40, No. 4 (August 1959), 251-265.

This Swiss scholar reviews the spate of articles that came out during the Cozzens controversy. He first gives an interpretation of *By Love Possessed* and intentionally avoids any evaluating comment. Straumann notes the many contradictions in the critical reception of the novel and chides many reviewers–American as well as British–for using arguments that are either not verifiable or refer almost entirely to non-aesthetic categories. "With one exception all the judgments passed on the novel are not based on any clearly definable and indisputable reasons. . . . These reasons are brought into focus to support some preconceived likes and dislikes."

C63 Tannenbaum, Earl. "Cozzens the Defender," *Saturday Review*, 40, No. 37 (September 14, 1957), 29.

Sets the record straight on the date of publication of "A Democratic School" in *Atlantic Monthly*.

C64 Tibbetts, A. M. "Possessed by Love, Death, and Taxes," *College English*, 19, No. 7 (April 1958), 318-320.

A pastiche of *By Love Possessed*.

C65 *Time*, 70, No. 10 (September 2, 1957), 72-74, 76, 78. "The Hermit of Lambertville."

For the most part a review of *By Love Possessed*, which the anonymous reviewer finds a good novel except for its style, which is overloaded with "parenthetical clauses, humpbacked

syntax, Jamesian involutions, Faulknerian meanderings."
Cozzens roots his novels solidly in the American scene but is
really alien grain in the American corn, for he is "classical, dry,
cerebral, . . . pessimistic, . . . temperamentally aristocratic, [has]
an age complex," accepts change but deplores it, and prefers to
contemplate life whereas Americans like to touch and handle it.
In *By Love Possessed* the theme is developed almost musically, "but
it is the austere music of a Bach fugue, architectonic, contrapuntal,
slow, majestic, sometimes irritatingly tedious, always impressive
if not steadily arresting." Thus "if the philosophical tension of
a Cozzens novel is always high, the emotional voltage is often
low." This article is also valuable for the biographical information
it provides on Cozzens as well as for some quotes that are
attributed to him and which one wonders whether to take at
face value or not, such as "I still feel I'm better than other
people" and "I suppose sex entered into [my marriage]. After all,
what's a woman for ?" and his various pronouncements on
Hemingway, Sinclair Lewis, Faulkner, and Steinbeck. Cozzens
later stated in a letter: "Defensive, I feel perhaps I ought to [say]
that crack in *Time* that so infuriated Macdonald about my thinking
myself better than other people was, let us say, a misapprehension
on the part of [the] *Time* man. . . . I'd got tired of silly
questions . . . . The dangers and failures of irony."

C66 *Times* [London], March 25, 1960, p. 11. "Man in the
News: The Shyest of the Literary Lions."

Announcement of the awarding of the Howells Medal of the
American Academy of Arts and Letters for *By Love Possessed*.
Notes Cozzens' deliberate isolation and his erudition. "His
theme is man in society. . . . He explores the limits set by what
is politically possible on the activities of men of good will."
Rates *The Just and the Unjust* his best novel.

C67 *Times Literary Supplement* [London], September 11,
1969, p. 1002. "By Cozzens Obsessed."

Half of this review of John William Ward's *Red, White, and Blue* [see C70] is devoted to remarks on Cozzens and was sparked by Ward's "absurdly high estimate of *By Love Possessed*." Cozzens is a good second-rate novelist who deserved a better climax to his career than *By Love Possessed*.

C68 Van Gelder, Robert. "James Gould Cozzens at Work," *New York Times Book Review*, June 23, 1940, p. 14.

An interview with Cozzens, who comments on the discipline to which he must submit himself "to express precise meanings, unshadowed by any falsity," on the mistake of publishing a novel when too young (*Confusion*), on collecting material for the novels, on the subject of *The Just and the Unjust*, then called *The Summer Soldier* ("about a lawyer who must make a choice between an ideal and what might be called a selfish, practical consideration"), and on literature ("the sloppiness of much contemporary writing").

C69 Van O'Connor, William. "A Muted Violence," *Critique*, 1, No. 3 (Winter 1958), 54-55.

Cozzens "creates a muted violence, like a depth bomb that ruffles the surface only a little. . . . His sentences are if not infelicitous at least undistinguished."

C70 Ward, John William. "James Gould Cozzens and the Condition of Modern Man," *American Scholar*, 27, No. 1 (Winter 1957-58), 92-99. Reprinted in his *Red, White, and Blue: Men, Books, and Ideas in American Culture*. New York: Oxford University Press, 1969. pp. 106-122.

Cozzens' mature work is about the condition of man, to which a limit is set by time and another by man's nature, which is divided between reason and passion. "To act in the full awareness of the irony of the conditions within which he must act is, for Cozzens, the dignity of man." Other related themes are the need for experience, the discrepancy between the ideal and the actual, the art of the possible, and the search for order in a disorderly world. Ward then explores the reasons why Cozzens suddenly became famous in 1957 with *By Love Possessed*. It is not that his themes and manner had changed; "Cozzens' fiction may be born of . . . the cause of a skeptical conservative who does not think too much can be done with the way things are. . . . It is probably true that more Americans can more readily share Cozzens' view now than ever before. Since the Second World War, high aspirations and heady ideals have come to seem somewhat embarrassing . . . to many Americans. So the acceptance of Cozzens today may be as much a function of the intellectual climate as was his neglect before." [See C38]

C71 Waterman, Rollene. "By Art Possessed," *Saturday Review*, 40, No. 34 (August 24, 1957), 14-15.
Biographical data.

C72 Watts, Harold H. "James Gould Cozzens and the Genteel Tradition," *Colorado Quarterly*, 6, No. 3 (Winter 1958), 257-273.

Watts argues that Cozzens writes as if the genteel tradition had never died; as it emerges from the later novels, "it is one of the few surviving bearers of rationalism in American culture. [It] is basically agnostic. [It] had and still has a real esteem for law." Its agnosticism is not militant, rather "it is protective of reason and the web of social and legal tradition." Even though Cozzens is aware of the "inadequacies of the genteel tradition as a total criticism of life," he maintains that it is worthy of study as a way of life that is in danger of disappearing. One restrictive comment: "Cozzens' 'world' is a world that has made and keeps on making . . . an intelligent, reasoned acceptance of the *status quo*," thereby implying that there are important questions that leave Cozzens and his heroes cold.

C73 Weaver, Robert. "The World of *The Just and the Unjust*," *Tamarack Review*, 5 (Autumn 1957), 61-66.

Deals with all of Cozzens' novels from *S.S. San Pedro* to *By Love Possessed*. Weaver describes the object of Cozzens' fiction as "one segment of American society" (the traditional professions), living in one part of the country, "the conservative, respected, responsible, somewhat aloof and autocratic" Anglo-Saxon Protestant American. The themes: "it is man's fate to live imperfect in an imperfect world, . . . a synthesis of a disciplined and aristocratic temper, a belief in the virtues of honor, loyalty, and responsibility." He also notes the unities of time and space. "Cozzens's style is now sometimes wordy, or pretentious, but it is effective in a compulsive, oddly irritating way." The novels have "downbeat endings."

C74 Weimer, David R. "The Breath of Chaos in *The Just and the Unjust*," *Critique*, 1, No. 3 (Winter 1958), 30-40.

The novel takes up the question of appearance and reality and to its main character falls the task of learning how to act in a world where appearances may deceive. The cardinal virtues in the Cozzens ethic are self-discipline, considered, controlled action, and compromise. Weimer equates Cozzens' and Hemingway's codes, for they "both argue the necessity of self discipline in a universe lacking an inherent rational purpose." *The Just and the Unjust* suffers from serious defects: some of the characters are a little too obviously meant to act as mere foils; Cozzens' language "unmistakably reveals his commitment to idea, restraint" and is often as uninteresting as "book-keeper's prose"; finally, Cozzens again fails to deal creatively and sympathetically with emotions.

C75 *Wilson Bulletin*, 4, No. 2 (October 1929), 50.

Biographical sketch.

Book reviews

Confusion

D1   C. B. O. *Boston Transcript*, April 9, 1924, p. 4.

"Style is deep-rooted. . . . Inventive faculty seems fresh and full."

D2   Carter, J. *Literary Review of the New York Evening Post*, May 10, 1924, p. 739.

"Incoherent, without form, purpose, or interest. . . . However . . . a book of considerable promise. Cozzens will do much better."

D3   *New York Times Book Review*, April 27, 1924, p. 14. "There Was a Lady."

Confusion is not just the theme of the novel, but it is to be found in the very way Cozzens writes. The characters other than Cerise d'Atrée have no life, the theme of love is just an old rehash with no new illumination. Cozzens' prose "isn't poor, but neither is it distinguished. . . . The novel, however, isn't bad: just unnecessary."

D4   R. B. F. *New Republic*, 40, No. 512 (September 24, 1924), 105.

Though Cozzens is at times too obviously well lettered and some of his characters are a little too glib, he "handles his narrative with an assured skill. He has an abundant sense of drama, and his climaxes rise sharply and vigorously from balanced, plausible situations."

D5 Shipley, Joseph T. "Confusion Worse Confounded," *Nation*, 119, No. 3081 (July 23, 1924), 100.

"Mr. Cozzens has worked cleverly," but his style is slipshod, and there are too many absurdities in the tale.

Michael Scarlett

D6 *Bookman*, 62, No. 6 (February 1926), 709.

"A stirring tale of the 16th century."

D7 *New York Times Book Review*, November 15, 1925, p. 8.

"Success in imitating the spirit of Elizabethan dialogue. . . . The author has caught the atmosphere of the time with notable felicity." Notes the anachronism in Marlowe's presence at Cambridge after the Armada.

Cock Pit

D8 Bramble, David. "Cuban Drama," *New York Herald Tribune Books*, October 7, 1928, p. 4.

"Lancy Micks . . . is one of the most admirably done characters in fiction during the last year. Ruth, his daughter, would be better if she were only allowed to be the least bit feminine." Bramble concludes that even if this novel will not create a sensation, its action and excitement will win many readers.

D9 D. L. M. "A Story of the Sugar Industry in Cuba," *Boston Transcript*, November 10, 1928, p. 5 (Book Section).

A story with a "full measure of excitement." But sometimes Cozzens explains too little and leaves the reader confused.

D10 Glenn, Isa. *New York Evening Post*, September 29, 1928, p. 9.

"A remarkable book to have been written by a young man. . . . A great love story told reticently."

D11 *New York Times Book Review*, October 7, 1928, pp. 28, 31. "Cuban Sugar Planters."

The novel has many exciting incidents and a dramatic plot developed almost entirely by action and dialogue; there is an abundance of drama and the characters are flesh-and-blood people. One objection: there is too little explanation for those who know nothing about the sugar business.

The Son of Perdition

D12 Bolitho, William. *World*, September 17, 1929, p. 15.

Cozzens has "arrived fully at [a high] level of skill in phrase and epithet, in the mechanics of description." But Bolitho deplores the use of violence and of "crapulous" characters which seems to be in keeping with a "dissatisfaction and a disbelief" peculiar to American literature of the 1920s.

D13 *Booklist*, 26, No. 2 (November 1929), 70.

"The deftness with which [Cozzens] mingles the ludicrous and the horrible reminds one of Stevenson."

D14 *Bookman*, 70, No. 4 (December 1929), XXVI.

"A novel of atmosphere and character rather than plot. . . . The characters are drawn with firmness and the word-coloring is rich."

D15 Cail, H. L. *Portland Evening News*, October 22, 1929, p. 8.

"A good novel, well constructed and rich in human character. . . . Evenness of tone, . . . picturesqueness, . . . deep understanding of human nature."

D16 J. C. G. *Boston Transcript*, September 4, 1929, p. 2.

Cozzens "has brought to view a vivid, realistic array of characters that cannot soon be forgotten."

D17 McFee, William. "Desperately Interesting," *New York Herald Tribune Books*, September 1, 1929, p. 2.

The Son of Perdition is "unconventional, . . . on occasion, realistic, impressionist and modern, with a dash of mordant mysticism. . . . It contains several almost-masterpieces of characterization. . . . [It] is an audacious and successful attempt to give elemental characters a genuinely modern treatment."

D18 Paterson, Isabel. "Big Business as the Protagonist," *New York Herald Tribune*, September 13, 1929, p. 16.

This novel gives the reader a "sense of unfulfillment of a curious and powerful talent." The themes are diluted and lack tension.

D19 Poore, C. G. "A Strongly Dramatic Tale of Cuba," *New York Times Book Review*, October 6, 1929, p. 7.

"A story of Cuba, primitive and unregenerate," with remarkable style and characterization. "One of the distinguished novels of the year."

D20 *Saturday Review of Literature*, 6, No. 26 (January 18, 1930), 659.

This novel "tells a story that is made to seem of extraordinary importance; its method [indirect, vague, subtly allusive with a tortuous narrative often inclined towards obscurity] is therefore justified."

D21 *Springfield Republican*, November 24, 1929, p. 7e.
"Sugar Mills of Cuba in 'Son of Perdition'."

D22 *Times Literary Supplement*, [London], November 14, 1929, p. 929.

The atmosphere is well suggested, a number of characters are successfully drawn, but the story lacks coherence.

S.S. San Pedro

D23 *Booklist*, 28, No. 3 (November 1931), 104.

"Unfaltering directness . . . great economy. . . . The characters are portrayed with amazing clarity."

D24 Clarke, Alan Burton. *Bookman*, 74, No. 5 (January-February 1932), 583.

"Probably one of the finest pieces of graphic writing produced in this country for many years. . . . A breathless, climactic tale of action and tenseness stripped of all sentimentalizing and movie heroics." It would "do credit to a Stephen Crane or a Joseph Conrad."

D25 McFee, William. "Stephen Crane Redivivus," *Saturday Review of Literature*, 8, No. 8 (September 12, 1931), 117-118.

" 'S.S. San Pedro' is a strong, darkly designed book, full of elemental vigor, [with] an almost aggressive masculinity, both in style and tempo." But McFee notes a few inadequacies in the psychology of the characters and in the description of the ship's structure of command.

D26 *Nation*, 133, No. 3458 (October 14, 1931), 407.

"This short novel . . . tells the story of a shipwreck in a manner which Conrad has made famous. In none of its passages is it so distinguished as Stephen Crane's 'The Open Boat,' either in writing or approach or effect. It is scarcely even dramatic or compelling, but it is not dull reading."

D27 *New Republic*, 68 (September 30, 1931), 189.

"Mr. Cozzens' short novel, or long short story, is a moving transcription of the 'Vestris' disaster. Its best feature is the sense it gives of the ship and the crew together as forming a collectivity, a single organism progressing moment by moment toward disaster. The principal flaw in the realistic narrative is the introduction of a doctor whose features strangely resemble a skull, who gives an uneasy sense of impending danger to everyone who sees him, and whose apparition on shipboard is obviously intended to be symbolic."

D28 Ross, Virgilia Peterson. *Outlook*, 159, No. 2 (September 9, 1931), 58.

"Cozzens does not indulge in the psychological speculations which lie so easily to hand. The little book is wholly objective; the treatment of the story is concrete, sharp, and final."

D29 Southron, Jane Spence. "A Strong Tale of Catastrophe at Sea," *New York Times Book Review*, September 6, 1931, p. 7.

A work of art full of "universal, human interest." The tragedy of the tale, which "raises it to classic proportion," lies in the fact that the disaster was humanly avertible. Southron also praises the humor, the irony, and, above all, the economy of the book.

D30 *Springfield Republican*, November 29, 1931, p. 7e. "Tale of Shipwreck."

"A gripping tale, powerful in description and admirable in restraint." The narrative, "moving as steadily and as rhythmically as the engines below decks," shows that Cozzens had excellent command of his materials and method.

D31 *Time*, 18, No. 9 (August 31, 1931), 47-48. "After the Vestris."

No critical assessment except that Cozzens does "a good job of writing."

D32 *Times Literary Supplement* [London], September 10,
1931, p. 680. "S.S. San Pedro."

Cozzens induces a state of feeling in the mind of the reader by
touches that are subtle but cumulative. But these emotions "are
not those of curiosity about a disaster that has happened but
those associated with a foreboding that it will happen."

D33 Tube, Henry. "Interference," *Spectator*, 220, No. 7290
(March 15, 1968), 332.

A short review of *S.S. San Pedro* and *Castaway* on the occasion of
their republication in England. They combine "compulsive
readability with shameless interference." *Castaway* is a *tour de
force* because Cozzens manages to "put his reader inside his
hero."

D34 Warner, Arthur. "Ship's Doom," *New York Herald
Tribune Books*, August 30, 1931, p. 12.

"Mr. Cozzens's descriptions are sometimes murky, but they have
dignity and a certain power."

The Last Adam

D35 Bessie, Alvah C. "Connecticut Town," *Saturday Review
of Literature*, 9, No. 27 (January 21, 1933), 389.

Bessie admires Cozzens' narrative talent but does not analyze it.
He finds that the novel is overburdened with details, many of
them ill-digested and having no ultimate or immediate bearing
on the course of the narrative, and that it lacks "a profoundly
human understanding, based in a final and complete
self-knowledge."

D36 *Booklist*, 29, No. 6 (February 1933), 180.

"Sound workmanship, a gift for story telling and a hearty,
unsentimental gusto for life are all apparent in this unusual,
realistic novel. . . . A full-blooded, racy novel."

D37 Brande, Dorothea. *Bookman*, 76, No. 2 (February 1933), 189-190.

Miss Brande stresses Cozzens' objectivity and detachment and feels that this novel gives promise of much better fiction to come. As a woman, she objects to the obscenity of some passages.

D38 Brickell, Herschel. *North American Review*, 235, No. 3 (March 1933), 282-283.

"Cozzens has written an excellent novel in *The Last Adam*, a book . . . which shows a quite remarkable insight into the whole workings of a New England community, with a doctor as the principal character. It is a hard-boiled book, or, as we used to say, realistic; very frank in spots, and without the overtones, perhaps, that go into still better fiction. But it is undeniably good reading, done with skill and effect, and of value as a record of an American small town. The author is a young man of versatile talents, and ought to be watched."

D39 Butcher, Fanny. *Chicago Daily Tribune*, January 7, 1933, p. 8.

"No signs of youthfulness in his work. . . . The attitude of a seasoned human being who accepts life as an intolerable existence which only intelligence can make tolerable."

D40 Chamberlain, John. "Small Town Life in Connecticut," *New York Times Book Review*, January 8, 1933, pp. 6, 14.

Views *The Last Adam* strictly as a novel of and on New England which achieves the "subtle task of assaying a hybrid culture in terms of all its components." It is not a *tendenz* novel, but it reveals "the secret of the land of the Pilgrims' Pride, twentieth-century style." Cozzens' sense of a whole community is acute: "social comedy, a profound indication of the *mores*, and excellent characterization in terms of floating thought, jets of random speech and casual action that combine to build up a whole person," a technique which Cozzens may have learned from English novelists of the 1910s like May Sinclair.

D41 *Forum*, 89, No. 3 (March 1933), vi.

"A sympathetic and good-humored picture of a [New England] village."

D42 M. F. B. "Dr. Bull Looks at His Quiet New England Town," *Boston Transcript*, February 4, 1933, p. 1 (Book Section).

Praises the veracity of the descriptions of the New England village. It is a book without climaxes, but its "polygonic picture [is] fair and true."

D43 MacAfee, Helen. *Yale Review*, 22, No. 3 (Spring 1933), vi.

There is in this novel too much "unrestrained reporting of minutiae" which does not impart the intimations of perception and feeling that characterize a good novel.

D44 Matthews, T. S. *New Republic*, 73, No. 947 (January 25, 1933), 301-302.

"Mr. Cozzens will have to be classed with Mr. Wells as a non-serious novelist. . . . He has not burst forth, as Kipling did, full-fledged; but he has shown the same flair for making a plain tale melodramatic, the same fatal inability to make a plain tale true."

D45 *Nation*, 136, No. 3527 (February 8, 1933), 156.

Cozzens' study of human nature is just a little too neat, he "gives us the feeling that he is neatly solving a theorem, with the Q.E.D. that there is after all a good deal of human nature in mankind. . . . What the story chiefly lacks is the element of surprise–not the unexpected turn of plot, but the turn of character, the pleasurable surprise of detail and individualization."

D46 Paterson, Isabel. "The Web of Communal Life," *New York Herald Tribune Books*, January 8, 1933, p. 6.

A realistic study of a social microcosm which is handled with excellent workmanship and structure. The main characters are "sketched boldly and firmly," and give, with the many others that appear in the novel, "a background, a sense of populousness." Miss Paterson deplores the "deliberate, unnecessary coarseness of occasional passages," but admits that this is in the fashion of the times since, in this particular work at least, Cozzens belongs to the "hard-boiled" school.

D47 R. W. N. *Springfield Republican*, January 22, 1933, p. 7e.
Stresses the authentic local color of the novel. *The Last Adam* provides "more than the average range of enjoyment" and warrants "hopeful expectation as to its author's future account."

D48 *Time*, 21, No. 2 (January 9, 1933), 71. "Dr. Bull."
Stresses the factualness of Cozzens' writings; he "has a Kiplingesque flair for dramatizing hard facts, a shrewd zest for making a plain tale move and glitter."

D49 Weeks, Edward. *Atlantic Monthly*, 151, No. 2 (February 1933), 14.
The Last Adam "is a warm-blooded, robust story, easy to like. . . . [It] passes in a series of rapid-fire 'shots,' sustaining the reader's attention more by variety and surprise than by steady development."

Castaway

D50 Benét, William Rose. "Gruesome Crusoe," *Saturday Review of Literature*, 11, No. 18 (November 17, 1934), 285, 289.
Though he admits that *Castaway* is a fascinating story that "reveals the sort of imagination possessed by the earlier H. G. Wells," Benét finds its main fault resides in its lack of identification of Lecky and in the absence of justification for his presence in the store.

D51 *Boston Transcript*, December 1, 1934, p. 4.

"A 'horror' story without the chills and fevers. . . . Finely written."

D52 Marsh, Fred T. "An Urban Crusoe," *New York Times Book Review*, November 25, 1934, p. 17.

Marsh deplores the inexplicability of Lecky's presence in the store; moreover, Cozzens, starting with a fresh and brilliant idea, has failed to allegorize it and has merely turned it into a modern *Castle of Otranto*. "We do not think he has succeeded in evoking the terror, wonder, mystery, the mood of reflection about inscrutable matters that this order of writing aims to evoke from its readers."

D53 Plomer, William. *Spectator*, 153, No. 5546 (October 12, 1934), 542.

"I take the book to be a fable, with the moral that modern man is made up of stupidity and fear and vague licentiousness and will get what he deserves, but as I believe him to possess other qualities as well, a past, and possibly a future too, my attention was not closely held."

D54 *Saturday Review* [London], 158, No. 4123 (November 3, 1934), 344. "A Robinson Crusoe Story Nightmare."

Recognizes in *Castaway* a variation of the Robinson Crusoe theme; more striking is Cozzens' truly frightening realism in his descriptions of the mental side of the picture. "There is no disputing the brilliance of its telling."

D55 Tilden, David C. "A Department Store Crusoe," *New York Herald Tribune Books*, December 16, 1934, pp. 15-16.

Castaway "plunges straight into a situation that strains credulity to the breaking point and makes exorbitant demands upon the imagination." Tilden objects to the inexplicability of Lecky's

presence in the store and of many of his acts. Lecky is a
caricature of Robinson Crusoe, but the outcome of the story
is exactly reversed. The meanings of the book dovetail badly
in the end, and the novel simply comes down to a mere "scene
of grisly horror." He admits that the style is remarkable.

D56 *Time*, 24, No. 22 (November 26, 1934), 66-67. "Crusoe
Nightmare."

"Author Cozzens unfalteringly directs a tale that might turn
comic if he did not keep it rigid with suspense."

D57 *Times Literary Supplement* [London], October 18, 1934,
p. 712. "Castaway."

Deplores the lack of "realism" of the book insofar as, if the
story is a psychological study of a Robinson Crusoe cast away
in a realm of plenty, why then is there no serious attempt to
break out of the store and to get into touch with the outside
world ? In addition, the book has a scientific precision which at
times becomes too technical for a work of fiction. Still, the novel
is "original," very well written, and an interesting and distinguished piece of work.

D58 See D33.

Men and Brethren

D59 Brickell, Herschel. *Review of Reviews*, 93, No. 2
(February 1936), 7-8.

The Last Adam was better; still *Men and Brethren* is "a skilfully
done piece of work. . . . Most excellent dialogue."

D60 Brickell, Herschel. "James Gould Cozzens Portraits
New York Clergyman and His Problems in Brilliant
Novel," *New York Post*, January 2, 1936, p. 15.

A work with "imagination, a great degree of technical skill, an understanding of people, . . . a flashing command of dialogue, . . . humor, . . . the grave tenderness of comprehension and sympathy, . . . incisiveness, . . . a feeling of authenticity."

D61 Britten, Florence Haxton. "A Hard Day in the Vicar's Life," *New York Herald Tribune Books*, January 5, 1936, p. 4.

Men and Brethren leaves Miss Britten "considerably bewildered" as to the author's intention. "Neither tract nor exposé nor realistic study, the novel, readable as it is in outward form, is irritatingly inconclusive in its final effect and for that reason lacks the gusto and decisiveness of the author's earlier work."

D62 Butcher, Fanny. *Chicago Daily Tribune*, January 4, 1936, p. 17.

Men and Brethren is "an adequate and an interesting novel, with a principal character unusual and intriguing, but it does not seem to me great literature." At any rate it does not have "the kind of validity and humaneness" that *The Last Adam* had.

D63 Connolly, Cyril. *New Statesman and Nation*, 11, No. 264 (March 14, 1936), 421.

Men and Brethren "is altogether vivid, exciting and unusual, and makes . . . a deep impression."

D64 Davis, Elmer. "Moving Picture of a Cleric," *Saturday Review of Literature*, 13, No. 10 (January 4, 1936), 5.

Concentrates on the complexity of the main character. No critical judgment of the novel except that "Cozzens is good."

D65 Dieffenbach, Albert C. and C. B. Palmer. "Mr. Cozzens Limns a 'Smart' Clergyman," *Boston Evening Transcript*, January 11, 1936, p. 3 (Book Section).

Dieffenbach praises the "realism" of the novel but laments the absence of "the other elements of genuine religion" and hence feels that Cozzens is unfair. Palmer views the book as a social commentary packed with feeling and human experience.

D66 Gibson, Wilfrid. *Manchester Guardian*, March 17, 1936, p. 7.

Cudlipp is "a shrewd, humorous, lovable character, whose most erratic-seeming actions are governed by a secure faith in the ultimate spiritual values."

D67 Hurley, Albert S. "Priest in Manhattan," *Christian Century*, 53, No. 6 (February 5, 1936), 228-229.

"The story runs swiftly; the conversations sparkle. There is not a dull moment in the book."

D68 Kingsland, Dorothea. "Men and Brethren," *New York Times Book Review*, January 19, 1936, p. 6.

"A remarkable portrait. . . . The stage management of the plot is so suave and sophisticated as to be completely beguiling. . . . Cudlipp is virulently alive." Cozzens was at the time still "fascinated by that species of personality which no cataclysm short of sudden death can alter."

D69 Kronenberger, Louis. "Ernest Cudlipp," *Nation*, 142, No. 3680 (January 15, 1936), 79.

Argues that Cudlipp is the novel all by himself, "a brilliantly integrated and authentic characterization."

D70 *Living Church*, 94 (February 22, 1936), 242.

Conjectures that, since the characters are so keenly sketched, they may correspond to actual people. But, "whatever gentle malice there may be in the portraiture, it is so good-natured that nobody ought to feel hurt."

D71 Mandeville, E. W. *Churchman*, 150 (January 1, 1936), 19.

"A perfect gem. . . . A *must* [for] everyone interested in the church and in the modern novel."

D72 Plomer, William. *Spectator*, 156, No. 5620 (March 13, 1936), 486.

"*Men and Brethren* has pace and sense, and I recommend it . . . to anybody who is interested in the Church's place in contemporary life."

D73 Schorer, Mark. "A New Parish," *New Republic*, 85, No. 1102 (January 15, 1936), 289.

Since there is little action in the book, this is essentially a novel of reflection. Cozzens "has the vital gift of growth"; *Men and Brethren* represents "a deepening of his work, an extension in stature as well as in scope."

D74 *Springfield Republican*, January 19, 1936, p. 7e. "Men and Brethren."

D75 *Time*, 27, No. 2 (January 13, 1936), 66-67. "Manhattan Parson."

"A highly interesting, racy book about faith and works. . . . Many an Episcopalian reader [will recognize] at least two likenesses–Bishop William T. Manning, onetime Father Harvey Officer–may think they see in his hero a similarity to the late Rev. Ralph Pomeroy."

D76 *Times Literary Supplement* [London], March 14, 1936, pp. 221-222. "Portrait of a Vicar."

The book draws a memorable portrait of a man on whose personality and vitality it lives. The characters "are projected upon the page as human beings embodying no thesis but only life itself, in a medley of action and motive from which, through Mr. Cozzens's unobtrusive, subtle, yet unquestionable skill, an authentic, if interrupted, harmony and beauty is eventually born."

D77 Van Gelder, Robert. *New York Times*, January 4, 1936, p. 13.

Praises Cozzens highly (''extraordinarily gifted as a writer, equipped with an almost flawless technique''), but has strong reservations about *Men and Brethren*, which is ''over-sexed and theme-ridden.''

D78 Walton, Edith H. ''The Book Parade,'' *Forum*, 95, No. 2 (February 1936), VI.

Written with ''considerable technical adroitness . . . *Men and Brethren* is neither so good nor so substantial a novel as *The Last Adam*, but it is ingenious and extremely readable.''

Ask Me Tomorrow

D79 *Atlantic Monthly*, 166, No. 1 (August 1940), n.p.

''Ellery is the guinea pig for the author's delicate, malicious, cynical satire. He is a brittle and futile young man, just as his creator intended him to be,'' which demonstrates another facet of Cozzens' versatility.

D80 Cross, Jesse E. *Library Journal*, 65, No. 13 (July 1940), 591.

''The plot is tenuous.''

D81 Daniels, J. *Saturday Review of Literature*, 22, No. 10 (June 29, 1940), 11.

''An historical novel'' and a ''flawlessly written story'' about American expatriates in the late 1920s.

D82 E. W. M. *Churchman*, 154 (July 1, 1940), 35.

"Very inconsequential."

D83 Fadiman, Clifton. *New Yorker*, 16, No. 18 (June 15, 1940), 93-95.

Cozzens is a good, honest, able novelist, but "he can't compete with a horribly accelerated history." His Europe is dead, so are his leisure-class American expatriates; but Fadiman admits that, given the time when the book comes out, that is hardly Cozzens' fault.

D84 Feld, Rose. "Youth and the Price of Life: A Sensitive Study of a Supersensitive Sophisticate," *New York Herald Tribune Books*, June 16, 1940, p. 2.

Cozzens knows the importance of the trivial and explores it with the fine hand of the practical artist. "As a story the novel is slight. But Cozzens is not concerned with plot and counterplot. He is concerned with human beings and the trifles that make them different and important."

D85 Gannett, Lewis. *Boston Transcript*, June 22, 1940, p. 3.

Not a good novel; "an anticlimax."

D86 Hawkins, Desmond. *New Statesman and Nation*, 20, No. 506 (November 2, 1940), 450.

A story that lacks ballast, but this is "compensated by the vivacity and polish of Mr. Cozzens' writing. . . . A brilliant portrait, charged with that rare wit which is both unsparing and compassionate." Hawkins likens Cozzens to Henry James for his irony, which is directed at the entire human situation.

D87 Littell, Robert. *Yale Review*, 30, No. 1 (Autumn 1940), XII.

"Cozzens is a novelist with considerable ability, but even more uncertainty as to what to do with it. . . . *Ask Me Tomorrow* is worth mentioning as an amusing study in tortured, self-conscious emptiness of soul."

D88 O'Brien, Kate. *Spectator*, 165, No. 5864 (November 15, 1940), 508.

Praises the verisimilitude of the setting and characters. The novel "is saved from sentimentality . . . by the impartiality of its bitterness."

D89 *Springfield Republican*, July 14, 1940, p. 7e. "Literary Egoist."

"Mr. Cozzens has capably portrayed a not uncommon character and cleverly reveals Ellery in all his moods and phases. . . . It is perhaps a question whether the significance of Mr. Cozzens' portrayal is equal to its ability."

D90 Thompson, Ralph. *New York Times*, June 13, 1940, p. 21.

A "quizzical, mordant, clever portrait." But, Ellery being the central character as well as the chief butt, Cozzens "has written a subtle kind of satire that, as satire, doesn't come off."

D91 *Time*, 35, No. 25 (June 17, 1940), 88, 90. "Collegiate."

Cozzens has not "outgrown his hero. . . . Skilled though he is as a craftsman, . . . [he] still shows a sophomoric taste for elaborate ironies and facetious quotations."

D92 *Times Literary Supplement* [London], October 26, 1940, p. 541. "Period Flavour."

Commends Cozzens' characterization, which is excellent, and his occasional wit. "This is very much a novel of the twenties, a little too literary in tone or sentiment and sometimes exasperatingly self-conscious, but nevertheless an honest and clever piece of work in its fashion of disillusioned egotism."

D93 Walton, Edith H. "The Portrait of an Egotist," *New York Times Book Review*, June 16, 1940, p. 7.

For all its humor, irony, and slickness of technique, there is something a little boring and "curiously footless and trivial" about this novel. It is a waste of time.

D94 White, Helen C. *Commonweal*, 32, No. 14 (July 26, 1940), 294.

The essential quality of the novel is that its young hero distinguishes himself by turning his frankness upon himself, which wins the reader's sympathy. The ending is a little inconclusive, a symptom of a certain formal weakness in the structure of the book.

The Just and the Unjust

D95 *Booklist*, 39, No. 1 (September 1942), 11.

A "serious, rather slow story. . . . Interest is divided between judicial procedure and small town life."

D96 Chafee, Zechariah, Jr. *Harvard Law Review*, 56, No. 5 (March 1943), 833-836.

Examines the novel strictly from the point of view of its legal realism and accurate evocation of trials and lawyers' lives. "One of the best legal novels. . . . The best account . . . of the daily life of ordinary lawyers." Its strength lies not in climaxes but "in the cumulative effect of [a] long succession of events and conversations." Cozzens has "imagination of a high quality."

D97 Chittenden, Gerald. "Crime Versus Local Misdemeanors," *Boston Globe*, July 22, 1942, p. 19.

Concentrates on an explanation of the novel's characters. Concedes that the trial is "not infrequently a little dull."

D98 *Christian Century*, 59, No. 38 (September 23, 1942), 1154.

This novel has a "lot of horse sense about human nature . . . and a pretty tenable and practical philosophy of law." Besides, "it is . . . a relief to have a novel . . . so skillfully written and with such an abundance of clever turns of word and thought, in which the element of romance is played down to an irreducible minimum."

D99 Fadiman, Clifton. "Just One," *New Yorker*, 18, No. 23 (July 25, 1942), 47-48.

"A careful, serious, rather low-pressured novel about lawyers and the law . . . full of that accurate, unbiassed characterization of more or less ordinary people that is Mr. Cozzens' particular forte. . . . A kind of small-scale 'Main Street'."

D100 Feld, Rose. "It's the Loudest Squeak That Gets the Grease," *New York Herald Tribune Books*, July 26, 1942, p. 5.

"Research, sincerity and a thoroughgoing examination of the ways of legal justice" have gone into the writing of this book, which displays "a quality of exact realism and sound reporting." Cozzens also does a remarkable job of portraying his characters; but for all this, the novel lacks spark and drama.

D101 Gibson, Wilfrid. *Manchester Guardian*, April 16, 1943, p. 3.

"A lengthy and somewhat slowly moving narrative. . . . [Cozzens'] overdeliberate manner of presentation tends to dissipate our interest in his carefully drawn characters."

D102 Gorman, Herbert. "Justice in an American Town," *New York Times Book Review*, July 26, 1942, pp. 1, 18.

A novel written with a "pervading sense of reality" by a major novelist; its real protagonist is justice as it is practiced in all American communities. Gorman stresses Cozzens' "fastidious abnegation of anything resembling an easy romanticism and his essential fairness and tolerance toward his characters."

D103 Hays, A. G. "Yankees in the Courtroom," *New Republic*, 107, No. 7 (August 17, 1942), 205.

Does not comment on the style or structure of the novel but likes "these plain, simple people who . . . make democracy work by rejecting the obvious histrionics for the compromised actuality."

D104 Hergesheimer, J. "The Conflict of Scruples," *Saturday Review of Literature*, 25, No. 30 (July 25, 1942), 5.

Insists on the quality of the illusions created by Cozzens, the mark of all good literature. *The Just and the Unjust* is "the source and form of unbroken pleasure . . . well contrived . . . reasonable and satisfying."

D105 Kinloch, Lucy M. *Library Journal*, 67, No. 13 (July 1942), 629.

"Double interest slows plot action, but the telling is realistic and characters well drawn."

D106 O'Brien, Kate. *Spectator*, 170, No. 5990 (April 16, 1943), 368, 370.

A carefully written, wise, instructive, and distinguished novel by "a writer with a despairing belief in the value of goodness, order and integrity, and who finds an ideal in men's attempts to understand and administer the laws which protect society." One flaw is that the central character's story is too much deliberated, not sufficiently lived: "he is a preposterously laconic Hamlet, too deprecatory by far, and an almost ludicrously dull lover."

D107 Prescott, Orville. *New York Times*, July 22, 1942,
p. 17.

In Cozzens' novels before *The Just and the Unjust*, "there was
something chilly; . . . a shrewd presentation rather than a warm
compassion. Something about them, a sort of intellectual
arrogance, deprived them of the power to stir the emotions, so
that their appeal was purely to the mind." One finds in *The
Just and the Unjust* the same former acuteness of observation and
restrained objectivity of manner, but also for the first time "an
undercurrent of tolerant understanding that seems very close
to a true and even gentle wisdom." The novel has a sound,
realistic wholeness of viewpoint, sharp flashes of insight, and an
inclusiveness that make it "a superb achievement."

D108 Sylvester, H. *Commonweal*, 36, No. 15 (July 31, 1942),
354-355.

A novel with "a sense of morality . . . and the strongest kind
of a sense of reality." A single flaw is its lack of emotion.

D109 *Time*, 40, No. 5 (August 3, 1942), 76-77. "Due
Process."

"As an unusually natural history of the public and private
behavior of lawyers, it is shrewd, entertaining, instructive. As
a study of the meaning and function of law and justice in an
average U. S. community . . . it is exciting and complex." But
Cozzens fails to dramatize the "tragically irreducible blend of
good and evil"; the book does not have "the slightest tremor of
human mystery. . . . Life is deprived of its splendor, law of its
dignity, society of its tragicomic stature." As a result, *The Just
and the Unjust* is Cozzens' best work and the year's most interesting
literary disappointment.

D110 *Times Literary Supplement* [London], April 17, 1943,
p. 185. "Law and the Free."

This novel excels in two ways: in its apparently complete and professional grasp of American judicial procedure–though characters come out credibly as individuals in spite of the profusion of legal technicalities–and in its "anatomy of American society in microcosm, a society held together . . . by a sentiment of liberty first and only next by a code of law."

DIII Weeks, Edward. "First Person Singular," *Atlantic Monthly*, 170, No. 2 (August 1942), 101.

Weeks praises Cozzens for "the almost effortless way in which [he] makes you identify yourself with a small Connecticut village. The novel's greatest quality lies in the interplay of law and life."

Guard of Honor

DII2 Becker, George J. "Men at War," *Commentary*, 7, No. 6 (June 1949), 608-609.

Though he admits that Cozzens is brilliant in some sections of the novel, Becker concludes that "the careful lack of focus, the persistent effort to avoid an issue, the deliberate reaching out to obvious and trivial episodes in the lives of the characters, become here a fundamental flaw, negating the very literary skill that is everywhere apparent. . . . There is a wealth of authentic detail, but the whole is a blur, a huge Delacroix canvas that becomes a little tiresome, no matter how engaging the parts."

DII3 *Booklist*, 45, No. 3 (October 1, 1948), 51.

DII4 DeVoto, Bernard. "The Easy Chair," *Harper's Magazine*, 98, No. 1185 (February 1949), 72-73.

Chides the "upper-caste literary critics" who have neglected Cozzens because he is not a literary man, but a writer. Admires *Guard of Honor*, for it reflects "wisdom, a deep sense of reality, and great skill."

D115 Gill, Brendan. "Zone of Interior," *New Yorker*, 24, No. 33 (October 9, 1948), 126-128.

"A compact and stringently disciplined . . . entertaining novel." A great novel of the year, but "not a great novel of our time," because of an absence of deep feeling and Cozzens' nagging failure to commit himself beyond irony. But it is Cozzens' masterwork.

D116 Goodale, Ralph. *Christian Century*, 66, No. 1 (January 5, 1949), 20-21.

Says nothing of the formal aspects of *Guard of Honor*, but praises Cozzens for his "knowledge of humanity." Yet Goodale suspects Cozzens of nursing shortsighted views about the issues that he dramatizes: he allows his characters to "treat the moral imperative quite cavalierly. A novelist with this creed will appear to one who disagrees to misinterpret moral idealism. And yet there is room in such a belief for intellectual vigor and wide understanding."

D117 Hillman, Serrell. "Three full days at Florida air base," *Chicago Sun-Times*, November 3, 1948, p. 59.

Praises the accuracy of Cozzens' descriptions of his professionals; he "has succeeded in capturing the spirit, as well as the day-by-day routine of the base." But he tries to encompass so much that individual scenes and characters do not stand out as they should; he fails to distinguish sufficiently between the important and the trivial.

D118 Jackson, Joseph Henry. *San Francisco Chronicle*, October 25, 1948, p. 14.

"Fiction of the first order."

D119 *Kirkus*, 16 (August 15, 1948), 405.

". . . building up to an unforgettable pattern. Cozzens writes with a taut violence . . . [and] with an expansive warmth."

D120 Maddocks, Melvin. "What Can or Cannot Be Done," *Christian Science Monitor*, 40, No. 260 (September 30, 1948), 11.

> *Guard of Honor* is a conservative book in which the author seems to find satisfaction in proving that there are no correct solutions, and that decision is more, rather than less, of a compromise. "Mr. Cozzens is expert at sketching a narrative and portraying character. From a less skilled writer, the none-too-profound emphasis on incapacity would seem crude. Humility is the handmaiden of wisdom, but to accept as 'facts' limitations that can be overcome–this is the one insuperable limitation."

D121 Meagher, Edward F. *Commonweal*, 49, No. 3 (October 29, 1948), 72-73.

> Meagher finds that this novel is overloaded with episodes and long-winded flashbacks that are, even though not entirely irrelevant, certainly not necessary to the main point. Cozzens writes "with the workmanlike wordiness of a Trollope whose lapses into gossip obscure an otherwise fairly engaging story."

D122 Munn, L. S. " 'Guard of Honor' Believable Drama," *Springfield Republican*, November 14, 1948, p. 7c.

> "An authentic and specialized account of top brass, civilian and career alike," distinguished by strength, maturity, and irony.

D123 Nichols, Lewis. "Wings over Ocanara, Florida," *New York Times Book Review*, October 3, 1948, pp. 5, 32.

> A precise reporter rather than an editorial writer, Cozzens "looks at his characters with warm understanding, with humor and with tolerance for their failings." His style is easy and flowing, with the underemphasis that makes for drama. But this novel "not infrequently drags." The characters talk too much and Cozzens talks too much about them.

D124 Poore, Charles. *New York Times*, September 30, 1948, p. 25.

> "Probing yet compassionate portraits." Cozzens "keeps his twelve-ring circus going with remarkable ease and expertness" and provides "quantities of suspense."

D125 Prescott, Orville. *Yale Review*, 38, No. 2 (Winter 1949), 382.

> Rates *Guard of Honor* perhaps the best novel of the year by one of the ablest living American novelists. Cozzens "creates all manner of intensely human and interesting people, involves them in complicated, natural, and fascinating situations, lets them speak at length (for themselves, not for him) in superbly colloquial dialogue." Only two reservations: the novel is a little too long and a little repetitious.

D126 Schorer, Mark. "You're in the Army Now," *New York Herald Tribune Weekly Book Review*, October 10, 1948, p. 4.

> Cozzens' best novel so far. Most impressive are his intimate knowledge of his subject, the "narrative movement which never flags and a dramatic interest always compelling and frequently intense." The real concern of the novel is power, the hierarchy of power, and the responsibility of power; General Beal is the dramatic center, Colonel Ross the thematic center.

D127 *Time*, 52, No. 17 (October 25, 1948), 110, 113, 114. "Human Odium."

> Notes Cozzens' "fine descriptive talents." The novel's main point is that "the world is far too wrapped up in different points of view for any one of them to be entirely true." This review's conclusion is a bit surprising in its wording: "Least of all, concludes Author Cozzens, does the big majority want the Negro to be fairly treated in wartime, because at heart it believes that in

a time of national crisis it is proper for the weak to be sacrificed to the morale of the strong, whose savage, intolerant instincts are essential to the prime aim–victory."

D128 Trilling, Diana. *Nation*, 167, No. 18 (October 30, 1948), 500-501.

One of the very few adverse reviews of *Guard of Honor:* "it is perhaps the most tedious document of the war effort that has come my way."

D129 Wasson, Donald. *Library Journal*, 73, No. 15 (September 1, 1948), 1192-1193.

"The intrigues . . . and the people . . . are brilliantly and accurately described."

D130 Weeks, Edward. "The Air Force in Training," *Atlantic Monthly*, 182, No. 6 (December 1948), 108.

In this "large-scale, very busy, very masculine novel," Cozzens offers us some of his best writing. But Weeks feels that it is not quite consistent as a narrative; though he respects the craftsmanship of many parts of the novel, he can only wish that *Guard of Honor* "were more of a whole."

D131 Woodburn, John. *Saturday Review of Literature*, 31, No. 40 (October 2, 1948), 15-16.

A "solid, supple, deeply-informed, and informing novel." Notable are Cozzens' ability to immerse himself in a profession and his extraordinary knowledge of people.

By Love Possessed

D132 Adams, J. Donald. "Speaking of Books," *New York Times Book Review*, September 15, 1957, p. 2.

"The most mature novel written by an American in many years." Notes in particular that in his handling of sexual episodes,

Cozzens "has succeeded in escaping the chilling touch of clinical detachment" and has restored a much-needed dimension to the treatment of sex in the American novel, "a department in which . . . our fiction has been notably deficient." But Cozzens fails to depict truly the "richer union of a mature man and woman who are moved by affection as well as physical desire," not because he is unable to do so but because, in Adams' opinion, it is impossible to do so. Adams concludes that Cozzens handles irony in such a way that he becomes "a little too wholly the observer."

D133 Balliett, Whitney. "*Saturday Review*'s Spotlight on Fiction: *By Love Possessed*," *Saturday Review*, 40, No. 34 (August 24, 1957), 14-15.

An ambiguous review. Balliett states that *By Love Possessed*, "a nineteenth-century moral novel," is "brilliant," its technique "almost forbiddingly finished," its author "the most mature, honest, painstaking, and technically accomplished American novelist alive." Yet his prose, "shaped in compact, baked, fastidious sentences," develops into "impossible log jams." Cozzens' "modern moral man comes perilously close to the superhuman" and the book is "part novel and tract." But Balliett admits that "Winner is the grandest moral vision in all Cozzens's work" though there are doubts about the novel's literary merits.

D134 Benchley, Nathaniel. "By Words Obsessed," *New Yorker*, 33, No. 51 (February 8, 1958), 100-101.
A biting parody of the opening pages of *By Love Possessed*.

D135 *Booklist*, 54, No. 2 (September 15, 1957), 44.
"An important and provocative novel. . . . Skillfully intermeshing time present and time past the rich, intricate, and disciplined narrative gives tangible solidity and depth to characters, place, and ethical issues."

D136 *Bookmark* [University of Idaho Library] (October 1957),
12.

"A remarkable novel . . . for mature readers."

D137 Bosquet, Alain. *Nouvelle Revue Française*, 9, No. 100
(April 1, 1961), 736-737.

Cozzens reminds the reader of Henry James because of his
descriptive realism and of John P. Marquand because of his
aristocratic ideas. He exposes all the qualities and defects of,
but is on the whole sympathetic to, a kind of reactionary
America. The novel, whose analysis of society is merciless, leaves
a lasting impression of power.

D138 Brounoff, George. *New Republic*, 138, No. 9 (March 3,
1958), 3, 23.

Finds that Irving Howe [see D160] misses the point in *By Love
Possessed*, the "final irony, the weakness of the men of reason,
[which] serves as a recognition that the moral life must never be
so inflexible as to destroy the human."

D139 Buckley, William F., Jr. "Gone Tomorrow," *National
Review*, 4, No. 16 (October 26, 1957), 380-381.

By Love Possessed is a bad book because it is a "grotesque
pastiche of tragedy, violence and sex that is passed off as
Realism"; it has "some of the most constipated prose in
contemporary literature"; it is weighed down with banal
observations; its attack on Catholicism is unfair and it is
humorless.

D140 Burns, John A. *Library Journal*, 82, No. 17 (October 1,
1957), 2451.

This novel, whose theme is the terrible havoc wrought by love
when it is not held in check by the steadying influence of reason,
"is slow and at times difficult reading, but it is always moving
and enormously stimulating."

D141 Burns, Wayne. "Cozzens vs. Life and Art," *Northwest Review*, 1, No. 4 (Summer 1958), 7-18.

A well-structured attack on *By Love Possessed*. Arguing (taking his arguments from D. H. Lawrence and Joyce Cary) that art, if it is genuine, can never be pretty or comforting, "can never leave us secure in our protective generalizations," Burns claims that Cozzens does exactly that in *By Love Possessed* and is therefore part of "the present cultural revival in this country [which is] almost wholly emasculative." The morality of *By Love Possessed* is a Norman Vincent Peale morality which has neither the penetration, the illumination, nor the consequent hurt and resistance that genuine art invariably generates. In other words, the novel is counterfeit art: "the fictional world it presents is in no sense creative; it is but a reflection of our conventional daydreams and rationalizations, set forth in big words and with artistic flourishes designed to make it look wide, and deep, and Tolstoyan." In short, Cozzens is a conformist engaged in comforting the upper middle class.

D142 Burns, Wayne. "Reiterations," *Northwest Review*, 2, (Fall-Winter 1958), 38-43.

In reply to Sherwood [see D182]. Elaborates on the points set forth in D141 and reiterates that Cozzens is, not anti-liberal, but anti-human.

D143 Butcher, Fanny. "Cozzens Writes Controversial Novel," *Chicago Sunday Tribune*, August 25, 1957, pp. 1-2.

Does not say why the novel is "controversial." Hints at the difficulty of the style.

D144 *Cleveland Open Shelf*, November 1957, p. 20.

"Considered by many critics to be the best novel of the year. Deals with two days in the life of a small-town lawyer, revealing how the various kinds of love can mold or ruin character."

D145 *Commentary*, 25, No. 2 (February 1958), 161-164.
Letters.

Of all the letters printed by *Commentary* in answer to Macdonald's
review [see D168], three are of particular interest. Albert
Friedman argues that Cozzens hardly qualifies as a "middlebrow"
but rather as a would-be highbrow writer. Saul Touster, a
lawyer, contends that the legal dilemma with which Arthur
Winner is confronted at the end of *By Love Possessed* is no dilemma
at all. Adam Yarmolinsky refutes some of Macdonald's
arguments. Macdonald's reply follows.

D146 Cowley, Malcolm. "The World of Arthur Winner Jr.,"
New York Times Book Review, August 25, 1957,
pp. 1, 18.

All of Cozzens' novels display a broad knowledge of human
nature and human institutions, a degree of professional
responsibility, an intricate pattern, and an easy style to read.
This is true of *By Love Possessed*, except for the style, which
"used to be as clear as a mountain brook; now it has become a
little weed-grown and murky," and has too many qualifications
and parentheses. *By Love Possessed* is not so brilliant as *Guard of
Honor*, but it goes deeper into human motives.

D147 Du Bois, William. "Forever Cozzens," *New York Times
Book Review*, September 29, 1957, p. 8.

Notes the phenomenal success of *By Love Possessed* and Cozzens'
reluctance to disclose his whereabouts and to allow his private
life to be brought into the limelight.

D148 Du Bois, William. "Recluse," *New York Times Book
Review*, August 25, 1957, p. 8.

A short interview by mail which is rather uninteresting except
for the tongue-in-cheek manner in which Cozzens answered the
questions (To "What is your favorite Cozzens novel?" he
replied, "*Confusion*. It seemed to me perfect when I was 19 and
nothing else I've written has ever seemed that way to me.")

D149 Durston, J. N. "A Great Novel by a Major Writer,"
House and Garden, 112, No. 3 (September 1957), 30-31.

An overly enthusiastic review of "a powerful, tremendously
moving new novel." Stresses Cozzens' masterful narrative skill,
his ability to draw characters, and the rhythms of his sentences,
which have a striking similarity to Faulkner's. Cozzens "is the
only remaining major novelist in the English language who is
utterly devoid of sentimentality," who understands sex and even
understands love.

D150 Einsiedel, Wolfgang von. "Zuviel der Liebe–oder
nicht genug ?" *Merkur*, 12 (1958), 681-685.

Written before the German translation came out. The title itself
points to one of Einsiedel's objections. The success of *By Love
Possessed* may be attributed to a wish among the public for a
return to a more "intellectual" and "artistic" form of literature,
and perhaps also (and unfortunately so) to a yearning for the
past, a defense of the status quo.

D151 Eimerl, Sarel. *New Republic*, 137, No. 13 (September 16,
1957), 17.

The plot is contrived, the characters sensational, and the style
heavy. But the "dramatic denouement" is effective. [See D162]

D152 Ellmann, Richard. "The American Aristocracy of James
Gould Cozzens," *Reporter*, 17, No. 5 (October 3, 1957),
42-44.

A balanced review. Surveys some of the novels (because Cozzens
"temporarily overlooked the upper classes [in *S.S. San Pedro* and
Castaway], . . . these are among his best works") and concludes
that "his theme is close to that of Conrad, the attempt to
practice virtue in a world that makes it difficult if not impossible
to do so. . . . [He offers] his hero only a choice among
expediencies." In *The Just and the Unjust* and *Guard of Honor*,
Cozzens "gripped firmly a succession of complex incidents, each

held tensely by itself and all in ultimate order"; they were
brilliant efforts to present a society. The style of *By Love
Possessed* "works well" in this continuation of "the saga of the
upper-middle-class Anglo-Saxon white Protestants." *By Love
Possessed* is pleasant to read, but it fails to pose a problem which
is really crucial and the ending is, in any case, not strong enough
to sustain it. Cozzens' solutions are "acceptably neat rather than
overwhelmingly necessary." The novel "suffers from being a
little detached" and Cozzens "walks away from us cool,
disenchanted, a little superior, pleased to have kept his distance."

D153 Fane, Vernon. *Sphere*, 233, No. 3030 (April 26, 1958),
146.

A short review that recognizes the technical excellence of the
novel's construction but finds Arthur Winner a "considerable
prig" and some of the physical details unnecessarily revolting.

D154 Fischer, John. "Nomination for a Nobel Prize,"
Harper's Magazine, 215, No. 1288 (September 1957),
14-15, 18, 20.

First lists the reasons why Cozzens had until then been neglected
by the critics and the public: he was a recluse who shunned all
publicity, his talent grew little by little rather than exploded,
and he was a nonconformist ("a classic mind, operating in a
romantic period"). Then lists the reasons why, according to him,
By Love Possessed is such an excellent novel: It is unsentimental
("it comes close to being the truth"); it is a work of classic
symmetry; no character is autobiographical; it has a powerful
feeling of suspense and excitement; and the ordinary reader can
identify himself with the characters. Fischer concludes the
review with the suggestion that Cozzens' corpus of fiction
should be proposed for the Nobel Prize.

D155 Fitch, Robert E. *New Republic*, 138, No. 6 (February 10,
1958), 21. Letter.

Disagrees with Irving Howe [see D160] on the grounds that "here we have, for the first time in a long, long while, the presentation of man as a rational animal–with the emphasis, as in Aristotle, on the rationality more than on the animality."

D156 Gardiner, Harold C. "Monument to Hollow Men," *America*, 98, No. 1 (October 5, 1957), 20.

There is a sense of mastery in the writing: it is "cerebral, penetrating and revealing," and the novel is monumental in scope and careful plotting. But its basic flaw is "a mistrust of life, a distaste particularly for the animal aspects of human life." The dialogue tends to be "tediously long and impossibly chiseled. . . . It is a monument erected to the inglorious memory of hollow men who dwell in a wasteland." [See B9]

D157 Gill, Brendan. "Summa Cum Laude," *New Yorker*, 33, No. 27 (August 24, 1957), 106-109.

One of the dithyrambic reviews. "A masterpiece . . . a bold and delicate book . . . an immense achievement" that reveals the "truth." According to Gill, "Cozzens has been superbly ambitious and has superbly realized his ambitions." Lashes at the "critics and the kind of readers who start fashionable cults" and the "psychoanalytic" critics who had neglected to give Cozzens his due even before *By Love Possessed.* Touches upon the main themes of *By Love Possessed* (mostly Arthur Winner's involvements and dilemmas), but says nothing of the novel's technique and style. Mentions "one sign of strain" ("the love of middle-aged couples many years married making love with a passion never known in youth") but otherwise praises Cozzens for scrutinizing love in all its forms.

D158 Harding, D. W. "The Limits of Conscience," *Spectator*, 6773 (April 18, 1958), 491.

Examines the themes of the novel in detail, in particular the theme of responsibility and the theme of love. On the whole

rather laudative ("Winner is used as a percipient of almost
Jamesian subtlety") but notes that Cozzens consistently ignores
one form of love ("a subtler intimacy between man and woman
achieved by way of sexuality") and that the novel suffers from
a "certain slowness and heaviness." [See D172]

D159 Hicks, Granville. "Traditional Novels by Gerald
Warner Brace and James Gould Cozzens," *New
Leader*, 40, No. 34 (September 2, 1957), 17-18.

By Love Possessed is "an event of considerable importance for
American literature"; Cozzens is committed and writes with
intensity. Praises the density ("the most elaborate and effective
kind of counterpoint") and the style ("without forsaking clarity
and correctness, he achieves great eloquence and even poetic
power. . . . A richness of literary allusion widens the implications
of the writing, and an unobtrusive, uninsistent use of symbol
points to deeper meanings"). The general point of view is that
of conservatism, but, since the defense of reason is central in
the book, it is rational rather than traditional conservatism.
But Cozzens also gives feeling its due, "so that a tension [between
reason and feeling] is set up that makes the whole richly
conceived, finely constructed novel vibrate with life."

D160 Howe, Irving. "James Gould Cozzens: Novelist of the
Republic," *New Republic*, 138, No. 3 (January 20,
1958), 15-19.

Finds fault with the themes and technique of *By Love Possessed*.
Agrees that Cozzens succeeds in the elementary task of creating
the illusion of verisimilitude, but finds that many of his novels
are overloaded with information about the professional activities
of their heroes, that secondary characters wilt into lifelessness,
that the leading characters are frequently sentimentalized, and
that, assuming the stance of the wilfully bigoted spirit, "Cozzens
has taken for himself the role of an irritated spokesman for the
values of a snobbish and soured rationalism that approaches

nineteenth century American Know Nothingism." Winner is a
mediocre figure, a prig, and the style of the novel is a mere
reflection of the "pretentiousness and emptiness and elephantine
coyness of Cozzens as a thinker." The only thing then that could
make the novel successful is its "Philosophy of Limit" which
states that "That is the way life goes and, man being what he is,
that is the way it must go." Not that this is anything new in
Cozzens, but "it is the weary *Zeitgeist* that has finally limped
round to him." [See D138, D155]

D161 Howe, Irving. *New Republic*, 138, No. 9 (March 3,
1958), 23-24.
Reply to Brounoff's letter [see D138].

D162 Hoyle, James F. *New Republic*, 137, No. 18 (October
21, 1957), 23. Letter.
Takes Sarel Eimerl [see D151] to task for his review of *By Love
Possessed*. Emphasizes that Cozzens' "vision of love is comparable
in many ways to the great medieval idea of charity. . . . *By Love
Possessed* is a novel of brilliant elegiac realism."

D163 Hughes, Riley. *Catholic World*, 186, No. 1113
(December 1957), 229-230.
The main features of *By Love Possessed* are its inflated writing and
bombast, an essential vulgarity, and a fundamental anti-intellec-
tualism. It is also "informed by a loathing of Catholicism; this
is the book's 'seriousness'; it *is* its meaning."

D164 John, K. "The Novel of the Week," *Illustrated London
News*, June 7, 1958, p. 984.
By Love Possessed is "wiredrawn, iterative, and magniloquent, but
it is superbly organized."

D165 Johnson, Jerah. *Carolina Quarterly*, 10, No. 1 (Fall
1957), 68-69.

Discusses Cozzens' "philosophy of limits" as expressed in *By Love Possessed*. Johnson's sharpest remarks concern Cozzens' style: "he is primarily a word man. He is not so much interested in sentence smoothness and readibility as he is in the right word. . . . He has taken the traditional approach of prose description and narration and polished it to a fine deep glow. The end product . . . is a calm, even, disciplined, exact, and tremendously powerful writing that carries a total effect not dissimilar to that found in the Classics." Cozzens' shortcomings are his often too obvious system of symbols and his frequent clumsy sentence structure.

D166 *Kirkus*, 25 (June 15, 1957), 421.

"A modern-styled novel. . . . The style is oddly diffuse, sometimes tortured, often oblique, and at times pictorial, vivid, dramatic. [Cozzens reveals] the buried emotions, the mental contrivings, the rationalizations, the confusion that combine to make up the whole man."

D167 Lister, Richard. "The American idol faces a crisis," *Evening Standard* [London], April 15, 1958, p. 14.

A very good novel and a "beautiful structure." But it is long, subtle and difficult.

D168 Macdonald, Dwight. "By Cozzens Possessed," *Commentary*, 25, No. 1 (January 1958), 36-47. Reprinted in his *Against the American Grain: Essays on the Effects of Mass Culture*. New York: Random House, Inc., 1962, pp. 187-212 and in *The Commentary Reader: Two Decades of Articles and Stories*, Norman Podhoretz, ed. New York: Atheneum, 1966, pp. 567-585.

The most famous attack on *By Love Possessed*, and probably the most unfair, though Macdonald makes several valid points. He first derides all the reviewers who went raving over *By Love Possessed* and then proceeds to say why, in his opinion, the novel "falls below any reasonable literary criterion." Cozzens' characters are guilty of an unforgivable lack of passion; where there is passion, as in sex, it is presented as implausible: "Cozzens is not so much cool as inhibited, not so much unsentimental as frightened by feeling." Cozzens' philosophy is cheap in the sense that all the book presents is a continuous rehashing of obvious truths couched in grandiloquent terms; moreover, Cozzens' fascination with the law makes him confuse it with philosophy. In addition, "the author is guilty of the unforgivable novelistic sin: he is unaware of the real nature of his characters," which leads him to make Arthur Winner a prig, unintentionally, of course. Macdonald's most direct attack is on the style: "Stylistically, *By Love Possessed* is a neo-Victorian cakewalk"; Cozzens has no ear for speech at all, and Macdonald categorizes the defects of his style as "Melodramatics," "Queer strangled sententiousness," "Pointless inversion," and "Toujours le mot juste." It all makes the novel a "pastiche in the manner of George Meredith." Finally, "*l'affaire Cozzens* indicates a general lowering of standards," the latest episode in "the Middlebrow Counter-Revolution" which has found a "pigeonhole for Cozzens: The Novel of Resignation." [See D145]

D169 McKernan, Louis. "Profile of an Aristocrat: James Gould Cozzens," *Catholic World*, 186, No. 1112 (November 1957), 114-119.

Does not think Cozzens attacks Catholicism but the sentimentalism of any religion. "Cozzens has not written a novel of prejudice; it is too existentialist, too involved in the dilemmas of the Man of Reason." But notes that the opinions expressed by the author in the novel are far more genuine than the tensions tormenting the soul of the central character.

D170 Maddocks, Melvin. "A Delayed Emergence," *Christian Science Monitor*, 49, No. 233 (August 29, 1957), 11.

Maddocks implicitly asks whether Cozzens deserves the enthusiastic, though late, acclaim he received from some critics.

He notes his Jamesian prose style, but finds that the novel's crucial flaw may be "Cozzens' artfully concealed refusal to deal with love in its fuller and more successful affirmations. . . . Readers may feel, in spite of [the book's] brilliance, the chill disappointment of having been exposed to love as an absence rather than a presence."

D171 Metcalf, John. "Great American Novel ?" *Sunday Times* [London], April 13, 1958, p. 8.

"A brilliantly assured display of technical skills. . . . An absorbing, moving, consummately professional piece of work." But its main character, meant as a hero, is a mere prig (Cozzens' "kind of moral myopia") and the style is often impossible.

D172 Millgate, Michael. "By Cozzens Unpossessed," *New Republic*, 138, No. 23 (June 9, 1958), 21.

Surveys some of the English reviews of *By Love Possessed* and notes that most of them were much less laudative than the early American reviews. Criticizes D. W. Harding [see D158] for reviewing the novel as a psychologist rather than as a literary critic and for overpraising its style.

D173 Nemerov, Howard. "The Discovery of Cozzens," *Nation*, 185, No. 14 (November 2, 1957), 306-308. Reprinted in his *Poetry and Fiction: Essays*. New Brunswick: Rutgers University Press, 1963, pp. 270-276.

Expresses his astonishment at the enthusiastic reception of *By Love Possessed*. Praises the novel for its discursive qualities but notes that the characters are stereotyped and that the book "suffers from a want of essential drama."

D174 Prescott, Orville. *New York Times*, August 26, 1957, p. 21.

A dithyrambic review. "No other American novelist of our time writes with such profound understanding of the wellsprings of human character and of the social pressures that help to inform it. No other American novelist writes technically more expert fiction. Mr. Cozzens is a master of dialogue, of flashbacks, of characterization, and of the special lore of numerous occupations. . . . This is a philosophical novel in the best sense. . . . Mr. Cozzens looks at the spectacle of human folly, ignorance, stupidity and irrational emotion with a sort of stoic wisdom and an almost Olympian compassion." However Prescott warns against "turgid and clumsy patches here and there [in the style], a disconcerting profusion of unknown words," and some prejudices against the Roman Catholic Church.

D175 Price, Martin. *Yale Review*, 47, No. 1 (Autumn 1957), 153-155.

By Love Possessed lacks the comic view; except for two scenes (Winner's interviews with Ralph Detweiler and Mrs. Pratt), it has little dramatic force; much of the dialogue is needlessly interminable; its philosophy is mostly trivial.

D176 Priestley, J. B. *New Statesman*, 55, No. 1415 (April 26, 1958), 533. Letter.

Disagrees with Richardson [see D178]. Admits that the book has been overpraised in the United States and does not like its "over-rational, anti-romantic, cold conservatism," but maintains that it is "an unusually massive and intelligent piece of fiction."

D177 Puffmore, Henry. "Under Review," *Bookseller*, 2731 (April 26, 1958), 1474.

A short survey of some British reviews of *By Love Possessed*. Notes that most British critics have objected to the length, the style, and the subject matter of the book.

D178 Richardson, Maurice. *New Statesman*, 55, No. 1414 (April 19, 1958), 510.

By Love Possessed is an "inflated mandarin pseudo-masterpiece [full of] nostalgia, a bogus philosophy of life, a constipated style." [See D176]

D179 Righter, William. *Epoch*, 8, No. 4 (Winter 1958), 251-254.

By Love Possessed is a novel of grand intentions that fails because it is less a work of art than an historical document. Cozzens portrays and admires a conservative, professional class, his "American image is a sort of conservative wish-dream." The characters develop into "the stock-figures of a morality." Arthur Winner is merely the author's spokesman, his Everyman; only the whipping-boys "have some semblance of an independent existence" because of the abuse they receive. Too often the book degenerates into a treatise or a sermon by a "moralist devoted to his message." The reader is overwhelmed by a deluge of unnecessary explanation and interpretation. "The novelist has sacrificed his realism to the requirements of a snobbish touch which creates unconscious comedy."

D180 Rivette, Marc. *San Francisco Chronicle*, August 25, 1957, p. 20.

"A major novel, even a great one. . . . A compelling journey of discovery."

D181 Schultz, Henry. *New Mexico Quarterly*, 27, No. 3 (Autumn 1957), 221-222.

Cozzens' finest accomplishment to date. The novel's chief qualities are an "absolute honesty in the examination of society, . . . utter integrity in the unfolding of character," and a plot that serves not merely to unfold a narrative but to reveal some truths about the human condition. "There are scenes of great brilliance and power to move." Notes, however, that "Cozzens has fallen victim to one of his own stylistic mannerisms –a sometimes maddening overuse of parenthesis, of qualification and overqualification of statement."

D182 Sherwood, John C. "Burns vs. Cozzens: The Defense," *Northwest Review*, 2, No. 1 (Fall-Winter 1958), 33-37.

In reply to Burns' attack on *By Love Possessed* [see D141]. Sherwood asks two questions: Is it true that whoso would be a novelist must be a nonconformist, and what is nonconformity? Since it is hardly possible to answer these questions, Burns' premises are put into question. Sherwood then shows that Cozzens is not in the least engaged in comforting the upper-middle class but rather in dramatizing the imminent collapse of the Brocton aristocracy, that he is "saying in effect that the world of Arthur Winner, the white, Nordic, Protestant, 'Anglo-Saxon' culture of which he is such an admirable specimen is . . . on the point of utter ruin."

D183 Shrapnel, Norman. "A literary life peer," *Manchester Guardian*, November 11, 1958, p. 4.

Cozzens "deserves some respect but doesn't seem the sort of writer to turn to when the home sap is running low."

D184 Stern, Richard G. "A Perverse Fiction," *Kenyon Review*, 20, No. 1 (Winter 1958), 140-144.

Dismisses *By Love Possessed* as a bad novel because its structural principle is badly flawed, "the expository devices are embarrassingly awkward and obtrusive, . . . irrelevant to an action but not to sheer panorama," the book is filled "with tortuous lucubrations," and the style is ambitious.

D185 *Times* [London], April 17, 1958, p. 15. "New Fiction."

"*By Love Possessed* is more of a conversation piece consisting of life-size figures drawn with the brush of a miniaturist than an eventful narrative."

D186 *Times Literary Supplement* [London], April 25, 1958, p. 221. "The Long Week-End."

Praises Cozzens' skill in organizing his material, but questions the novel's "tarnished verbiage" and the reality of the dilemma at the end.

D187 *Times Weekly Review* [London], April 24, 1958, p. 12. "New Conception of the Unities."

Cozzens uses a formal, fluent dialogue, but he is "a humorless, nineteenth-century schoolmaster, provincial in his ideas."

D188 Wagenbach, Klaus. "Den Schild der Worte um die eigene Blösse stellen, . . ." *Der Monat*, 12, No. 137 (February 1960), 76-78, 80-85.

Objects to everything in *By Love Possessed* but its structure ("der Aufbau [ist] gut, beängstigend perfektionistisch konstruiert"). But the style is atrocious and Winner's, and hence Cozzens', "analyses" are but hair-splitting digressions. Attributes the novel's sudden and short success to its appeal to a segment of the American public ("eine selbstgerechte und deswegen intolerante Masse") which could identify its own anti-minority feelings in the book, a political rather than a literary phenomenon. Wagenbach is the only critic to note a few discrepancies and inaccuracies in *By Love Possessed ;* also states that the translator knows neither English nor German.

D189 Weeks, Edward. "The World of Arthur Winner," *Atlantic Monthly*, 200, No. 3 (September 1957), 82.

Stresses Cozzens' persuasive manner that makes the reader sympathize with Arthur Winner's "strong current of personality. . . . This is a wise and compassionate novel, and I will not mar its enjoyment if I add that Mr. Cozzens dismisses the children in it rather perfunctorily and that his sentences, particularly where he is tempted to overindulge in the parenthetical, are sometimes confusing."

D190 West, Jessamyn. "James Gould Cozzens' Rich, Wise, Major Novel of Love," *New York Herald Tribune Book Review*, August 25, 1957, p. 1.

This novel has to do with the various kinds of "love" and with "human relatedness," with man in society (a relief in the face of so much current alienation in fiction). In addition, "this is a world, not a dream, and it has the coherence and plausibility of the rational." The reader may come to the end of the book with a certain degree of tiredness: "The involvement has been that complete, the issues at stake that significant."

D191 Wilson, Angus. "Back to Galsworthy," *Observer*, 8702 (April 13, 1958), 17.

A novel written by a very self-conscious reactionary, whose manner, point-of-view, and matter belong to the last century. Cozzens' greatest gift is his constructive power, a "brilliant interlocking of the numerous parts into a well-shaped, meaningful whole." But what Cozzens has to say is tedious and pretentious and it is couched in a "peculiar, difficult and pretentious idiom." Winner is a know-all and a prig; his wisdom is too often platitudinous or irrelevant to modern life, his sympathy seems "patronage or . . . even callousness," his humor is "a clumsy, heavy-handed sneer. . . ." There is also too much prejudice against Jews, Catholics, immigrants, youth, etc. This is what makes Wilson conclude that Cozzens' "true Americanism . . . is not just the old Bostonianism, but a neo-Conservatism with more sinister undertones of prejudice."

D192 Wyndham, Francis. *London Magazine*, 5, No. 7 (July 1958), 72-73.

A scathing appraisal of the novel. *By Love Possessed* does not have a message, nor is it a work of art. It is a "heavy-handed and pretentious" piece of fiction that suffers from a "ponderous, relentlessly repetitive style." Its only quality is that "it is well, and elaborately, constructed," but that, Wyndham says, "should really be taken for granted in an age when competition has raised the standard of professional efficiency."

Children and Others

D193 *Booklist*, 61, No. 3 (October 1, 1964), 132.

> "Uneven in style and impact but interesting as an index to Cozzens' development as a writer."

D194 Burns, Richard K. *Library Journal*, 89, No. 15 (September 1, 1964), 3183.

> "Mr. Cozzens . . . is a master of commonplace dimensions. Sometimes epigrammatic and often reminding one of a grammarian, Cozzens's writing is, nonetheless, well endowed with texture, timing and technique."

D195 *Choice*, 1, No. 11 (January 1965), 477.

> "Smooth, solemn, not very significant stories."

D196 Crews, Frederick C. "A Little Corner of the Status Quo," *New York Times Book Review*, August 2, 1964, pp. 1, 20.

> Notes first that the popular acclaim for *By Love Possessed* appears to have been a kind of mass delusion; at best the book was "rather a rallying point for literary and social conservatives," written as it was by a man who, as "a classic American stand-patter, not a Man of Reason but an apologist for his own little corner of the status quo," was a cultural symbol for the 1950s. In addition to its clogged rhetoric, the novel was marred by an infusion of a pedantic worship of the established power embodied in its hero. Cozzens is not much better in *Children and Others*, but for different reasons: he lacks a "precision of style and a knack of seizing character in abbreviated flashes of insight" which short fiction demands. [See D200]

D197 Dolbier, Maurice. "A Dozen Good Stories," *New York Herald Tribune*, July 29, 1964, p. 19.

Only the first three sections of the collection are good; the rest
is a let-down, especially "Eyes to See," which is "dull,
repetitious, unpleasant, and occasionally unbearably coy."

D198 Grauel, George E. *America*, 3, No. 9 (August 29, 1964),
218.

These stories give a representative view of Cozzens' conservative
themes, technical traditionalism, and interest in white, Protestant,
upper-middle-class mores. Cozzens "lacks the boldness of the
experimenter, the warmth of the romantic, and the leadership
of the true intellectual. His writings all too often degenerate
into melodrama and pathos."

D199 Hamilton, Alex. *Books and Bookmen*, 10 (July 1965), 31.

The people are real, the situations piquant, the style often
aphoristic and amusing; but Cozzens, consistently giving up the
chance of a dramatic ending, "is just about the most perverse,
self-defeating teller of short stories I have ever come across."

D200 Hart, Jeffrey. "By Ideology Possessed," *National
Review*, 16, No. 38 (September 22, 1964), 825-826.

According to Hart, the people who are "by ideology possessed"
are Frederick C. Crews [see D196] and Jean Stafford [see D210],
who reviewed the book unfavorably on, he charges, ideological
grounds. Though Hart states that "Eyes to See" "is written in
uncommonly lucid, though formal prose," and that some stories
possess "lyrical tenderness" and deal, "honestly and movingly,
with adolescence," he fails to demonstrate convincingly why
they are good stories. He is more persuasive when he defends
Cozzens' awareness of social class.

D201 Hicks, Granville. "Adventures into Awareness,"
Saturday Review, 47, No. 31 (August 1, 1964), 23-24.

Hicks wrote an enthusiastic review of *By Love Possessed*. He
admits, however, that the short story is not Cozzens' forte, for

"he rarely rises above the level of competent craftsmanship" in this genre: "there are many fine perceptions but no one blinding revelation." Finally he notes an "absence of emotional power" in the stories as in the novels.

D202 Lynch, William J. *Best Sellers*, 24, No. 9 (August 1, 1964), 165-166.

The rating Lynch gives *Children and Others* is "recommended." Praises Cozzens' "control, insight and stylistic precision. . . . There is a deliberate, rational handling of his characters, which permits him to see them unemotionally and critically, almost as an outsider. Orthodox in style and content, his writing flows smoothly and easily."

D203 Moynahan, Julian. "Only in America," *New York Review of Books*, 3, No. 2 (September 10, 1964), 14.

Dismisses *Children and Others* as a bad book whose writing is as stiff and flat as a board. Cozzens "writes badly: that is, with a very uncertain grasp of either English or American prose idiom and syntax." Furthermore Cozzens settles here for "conventional middle-class reticence and threadbare pieties"; the book is a mere collection of stock ideas and stock responses.

D204 *Newsweek*, 64, No. 6 (August 10, 1964), 69. "By Childhood Possessed."

Finds *Children and Others* a relief after *By Love Possessed* and, calling it a "fine piece of work, a simple pleasure," goes so far as to compare Cozzens to John O'Hara and Scott Fitzgerald at his best. Their common theme: "human flaw and weakness, sometimes undiscovered, sometimes suppressed, always there."

D205 *New Yorker*, 40, No. 25 (August 8, 1964), 90-91.

A "collection of uncolored, well-mannered fragments."

D206 Prescott, Orville. "The Short Stories of James Gould Cozzens," *New York Times*, July 29, 1964, p. 31.

Prescott admires Cozzens: he is "one of the few unquestionably major American novelists of this century. No other novelist I know of has written with such insight and truth about life as it is lived by upper- and middle-class people in this country. . . . [Cozzens makes a constant effort] to be impersonal, to be dispassionate although sympathetic, to understand without involvement." Though the stories in *Children and Others* display the irony, the worldly wisdom and the deadly penetration into individual character and into social environment that are Cozzens' specialities, they fall short of the quality which Cozzens achieved in some of his novels: "Mr. Cozzens is more impressive as a novelist than as a writer of short stories."

D207 Price, R. G. G. *Punch*, 248, No. 6502 (April 21, 1965), 602.

The best stories are those that deal with the closed community by which Cozzens has been fascinated since his early successes. Price does not pronounce Cozzens a middlebrow entertainer or a great man, but he points out that his faults should not detract from his many virtues.

D208 Pritchett, V. S. "Respectability," *New Statesman*, 69, No. 1779 (April 16, 1965), 615-616.

Respectability is Cozzens' subject: "he is *for* the old Calvinist Establishment down to the last drop of family suffering; his pessimism is masochistic and bitter." Pritchett's fundamental criticism of the stories is the very overtone of reminiscence that pervades all of them: "because they are *remembered*, his people never quite get off the ground as they do in the highest class of imaginative writing." Still, Cozzens "is remarkable in a difficult art, a master not only of form, but of a variety of styles." Singles out "Eyes to See" as a very accomplished piece of irony.

D209 *Saturday Review*, 49, No. 51 (December 17, 1966), 36.

Brief comments on the paperback edition of *Children and Others*. "A collection of short stories whose common denominators of sturdy plot and vigorously moral characters are only to be expected by the author of *The Last Adam* and *By Love Possessed*."

D210 Stafford, Jean. *New York Herald Tribune Book Week*, August 2, 1964, p. 5.

"Homogenized, inoculated for life against real adventure or real scandal, real anguish or real delight, [the characters] decorously romp and guardedly travail in a world-wide Westchester County." [See D200]

D211 Sullivan, Richard. "A Distinguished Novelist Out of His Metier," *Chicago Sunday Tribune*, *Books Today*, August 2, 1964, p. 5.

These stories are dull, written in "slow prose," and "they plod, craftily."

D212 *Time*, 84, No. 6 (August 7, 1964), 90. "The Little Men."

Sees in *Children and Others* another expression of Cozzens' "same unsmiling, nonextremist conservative" attitude, which dismisses the rebel in favor of the structure itself: "Childhood itself is the villain in these stories, and the thoughts of youth are wrong, wrong thoughts." Though the total effect of these stories is "oddly stiff and pathetic in a surely unintentional way," they can still be read as thoroughly enjoyable entertainments.

D213 *Times* [London], April 8, 1965, p. 15. "New Short Stories."

Cozzens is at his best in his Durham School stories, the most impressive being "The Guns of the Enemy."

D214 *Times Literary Supplement* [London], May 6, 1965, p. 356. "The Artless and the Arch."

Notes that Cozzens is better when working on a large canvas but still finds all the stories "beautifully shaped and full of meat." "Eyes to See" is much the best.

D215 Ward, John William. "Growing Up Rich," *Reporter*,
31 (September 10, 1964), 53-54.
These stories build up to what has come to be Cozzens' major
theme: "what it is to grow up and be a man." All the stories are
good pieces except "Eyes to See," which fails because of a
mismanagement of point of view and some confusion about the
meaning of the climax.

D216 Wardle, Irving. "A Dream of Youth," *Observer*
(April 4, 1965), 26.
"Many of the stories expire on a weary submission to the *status
quo:* which wouldn't matter if the writing itself didn't suffer
from the same lack of energy."

D217 Weeks, Edward. *Atlantic Monthly*, 214, No. 2 (August
1964), 114-115.
Weeks admires Cozzens' ability to catch the novelty of experience,
the power of his characterization, "the subtlety with which his
sympathy lights up the ancient conflict between the old and
young, . . . the value which he places on integrity."

D218 Weidman, Jerome. "Raise the Banner Again for
Cozzens," *Life*, 57, No. 6 (August 7, 1964), 9, 12.
These stories are "superb pieces" which all bear the "indelible
imprint of the Cozzens intelligence." Using sentences put
together with the precision of a Swiss watch movement, Cozzens
tells us "what only great writers of fiction can tell us: this is the
way life is, not the way we would like it to be." The Cozzens
drama is that people raised to believe that they are better, are
constantly surprised to discover that they are not really better.

Morning Noon and Night

D219 Anderson, H. T. *Best Sellers*, 28, No. 11 (September 1,
1968), 216-217.

Though Anderson admits that "Mr. Cozzens' craft is superb, his concept in the novel and his approach to it . . . both masterful," he dismisses *Morning Noon and Night* as a "polished, genteel, but classically boring book. . . . Everything seems to have been meticulously purged of every conceivable item that would make it interesting."

D220 *Booklist*, 65, No. 2 (September 15, 1968), 102.

D221 Brooks, John. "The I in Henry Dodd Worthington," *New York Times Book Review*, August 25, 1968, pp. 3, 33.

Morning Noon and Night "makes clear beyond cavil its author's austere, magisterial, almost relentless disregard for literary fashion." It may intend to be a searching study of the Puritan heart and mind, but it is marred by several flaws: "a tendency to laughably clinical exactitude" on the subject of sex, a prose style which is eccentric in the extreme and which creates an effect of archness and pomposity, a high unevenness in wisdom content, and a sense of chronic embarrassment which was certainly not meant to be included in the book. The reviewer also detects "more than a hint of a personal testament" on Cozzens' part.

D222 *Choice*, 5, No. 10 (December 1968), 1304.

"A minor performance masquerading as a major one" which continually shifts "from cynicism to *Weltschmerz* to unconvincing hopefulness in the authorial voice."

D223 Davenport, Guy. "Parables from Inside," *National Review*, 20, No. 46 (November 19, 1968), 1172-1173.

Even though Cozzens' portrait of an elderly American businessman is as true as life and an honest account of an old man's bemused tranquility, the whole thing is still very insignificant. Does Worthington not know, Davenport asks, "that there's more to life than money and revery ?"

D224 Freedman, Richard. "The Thinking Man's John O'Hara," *Washington Post Book World*, September 8, 1968, p. 3.

Freedman recognizes that Cozzens can be an excellent writer on occasion (witness *Guard of Honor*), and that he is an intelligent, hard-headed man and a serious craftsman, but wonders what has gone wrong since *Guard of Honor*. The style of *Morning Noon and Night* is pompous, inflated, and dispiriting; the hero is a "perfect stuffed shirt" and the novel itself full of "all the dismally banal Cozzens prejudices" against sex, F. D. R., liberals, and minorities. "The real trouble with the novel is that nothing the hero does or thinks is of remotely comparable importance to the exalted language in which his life is couched."

D225 Fremont-Smith, Eliot. "Keeper of the Flame, R.I.P.," *New York Times*, August 20, 1968, p. 39.

Morning Noon and Night is a "sleeping pill," written in a "coagulated, slow-motion syntax" which one scans "with increasing myopic urgency for clear indications of meaning, direction, intention, point, reasons for continued labor." Worthington is singularly uninteresting; the only tension in the book is not between the narrator and the people in his life, not even between his various observations and self-evaluations, but between him and the author, which gives the reader a strange feeling of being left completely out of the process.

D226 Fuller, Edmund. "World of the WASP," *Wall Street Journal*, August 29, 1968, p. 10.

An enthusiastic review of "one of the best novels" Fuller has read recently. The opening section is brilliant; the style, though at times a little tortured, is "always literate and [has] a rare range of vocabulary"; discursiveness and digression, though perhaps overdone sometimes, are among the book's pleasures. In a "humane but unsentimental, skeptical but not cynical, frequently funny" way, Cozzens is concerned with "the ancient problem of knowing the truth" and of how to state it.

D227 Hackett, Alice P. *Publishers' Weekly*, 193, No. 25 (June 17, 1968), 59.

"A thoughtful perusal" will reward the reader with the "intellectual and even emotional satisfaction that good books evoke." There is wit and warmth in abundance in this novel, which is written in a difficult style by a "man in a total environment that seems historically separate from today's world."

D228 Hicks, Granville. "Three Stages of Life," *Saturday Review*, 51, No. 34 (August 24, 1968), 33-35.

A rather embarrassed review by a man who admires Cozzens because "within his range, he sees people clearly and at a considerable depth." Hicks concedes that the novel has little action and that it moves slowly, that Cozzens devotes too much time to minor characters, and that the main character often sounds like a "pompous snob." He also finds fault with the style and Cozzens' fondness for unusual words. His defense of the novel is only half-hearted ("If we believe [Henry Worthington] exists, it does not matter whether we like him or not"), and such statements as "It is good Cozzens, and good Cozzens is never to be ignored" are hardly persuasive. Only the conclusion to Hicks' review carries some convincing power: "Cozzens . . . regards the absence of urgency as a virtue, but that is one of many indications that his world is not the world in which most of us live. He is a writer of integrity, thoughtful, scrupulous in his craftsmanship, . . . but there are other writers who seem to me to have more to say that is relevant to my life."

D229 Jackson, K. G. *Harper's Magazine*, 237, No. 1421 (October 1968), 109-110.

An ambiguous review that praises the "particular immediacy, [the] detail of the fabled recollections, the thousand threads in the fabric [that] mesmerized and delighted [the reviewer]," who then got bored by the elderly Henry Worthington. The story is good enough, Jackson says, but one is occasionally conscious of false notes.

D230 Junker, Howard. "Beginning to Flag," *Newsweek*, 72, No. 9 (August 26, 1968), 86, 86D.

Junker finds that Cozzens' talent is evaporating. Worthington employs, in setting down a few incidents from his life with little dramatic point, "a narrative style [which] is ineptly chaotic. . . . Too much is unstated or simply smothered in the apologies and tortured, abstracted meanderings of a narrator who recognized early on that he lacked a 'writer's temperament'."

D231 Kauffmann, Stanley. "Aimez-vous Brahmins ?" *Atlantic Monthly*, 222, No. 3 (September 1968), 119-121.

One of the most unfavorable reviews. Notes that Cozzens departs from his usual manner in the use of the first person and in the use of a narrative method of seemingly random memories. Kauffmann strongly objects to the "Brahmin pathos" that pervades the novel, to the lack of a story, to the "crinkum-crankum" style, to the hero, who is "a transparent fraud, . . . a hollow papier-maché figure containing the author," to the "spuriously humble note of apology throughout the book," to Cozzens' view of sex, and finally to Cozzens' conservatism, which "now superficial and anachronistic, merely laments the end of Anglo-Saxon dominance in America, a purely tribal dominance."

D232 Kenney, Edwin J., Jr. "The Stages of Wasp Man," *Nation*, 207, No. 7 (September 9, 1968), 218-220.

"A radical departure from the manner of [Cozzens'] earlier fiction." Dismisses *Morning Noon and Night* as a bad novel for the following reasons: It lacks the unities, the concreteness and immediacy that are Cozzens' greatest achievement as a novelist;

the book hardly conveys any "sense of an active inner life at all" in its hero, who never reaches any true sense of life or understanding of it; the rhetoric is "repulsively turgid, stuffed to bursting with badly chosen, misunderstood commonplaces from literature"; if irony is there, it is misdirected and it backfires; and the book is too much of a social and political tract.

D233 Levensohn, Alan. "A nonstop monologuist and his past," *Christian Science Monitor*, 60, No. 251 (September 19, 1968), 13.

Levensohn's thesis is that *Morning Noon and Night* is a blend of autobiography and fiction; he proves it rather convincingly by drawing several parallels between Cozzens and Worthington. The utter failure of the novel is due to Worthington's unpleasantness and blind vanity. The "old man's rage," which emerges off and on, "is only a strangulated undercurrent, betraying itself too infrequently to maintain the reader's interest." As he concludes, "to the extent to which the book is Cozzens' own memoir, its over-guardedness is, if . . . understandable, still more to be regretted." The main flaw is, again, an absence of feeling.

D234 Lindroth, James R. *America*, 119, No. 5 (August 31, 1968), 136.

One of the few entirely favorable reviews of *Morning Noon and Night*, which is a "tour de force of complex structure and challenging insights," though Lindroth notes that the structural principle is uncommonly difficult. The high quality of the novel is due to Cozzens' technical virtuosity and to the "overwhelming sense of the power of life to be found here, and of the vast richness that even the quietest individuals experience. Furthermore, *Morning Noon and Night* is "a memoir of a good part of middle class American society." Finally, "through the numerous literary references that become a part of the novel's very framework,

Cozzens implies that the history of Worthington is, in its own quiet way, the history of Western Everyman."

D235 Maddocks, Melvin. "The Absentheartedness of Mr. Cozzens," *Life*, 65, No. 9 (August 30, 1968), 6.

Morning Noon and Night is a very disappointing novel because, on the one hand, neither Worthington nor Cozzens is genuinely interested in people, and, on the other, because Cozzens "will not or cannot get to the real point. He clears his throat."

D236 Ridley, Clifford A. "Mr. Cozzens and Mr. Horgan: Two Deal With the Past, With Contrasting Results," *National Observer*, 7 (September 9, 1968), B7.

A favorable review. Says very little about the "philosophy" of Henry Worthington, but praises the technique of the book (the lack of chronology or structure) which "becomes a recurring symbol of growth and change." Ridley is enthusiastic about the novel's style: "Clauses and sentences succeed one another with the propulsive inevitability of the surf, yet conceal within them eddies and pauses and subtle changes of direction that keep us simultaneously seeking the ripples as we marvel at the relentlessness of the waves." Admits that one has the feeling that it is Cozzens who is speaking in the novel through Worthington. In short, *Morning Noon and Night* "is a very good novel, highly recommended."

D237 Ringer, Agnes C. *Library Journal*, 93, No. 13 (July 1968), 2688.

Because of Cozzens' substantial gifts of intellect, style, and technical brilliance, this novel "of undeniable worth . . . further establishes him as one of the major novelists of our time."

D238 Thompson, John. "Return of the Repressed," *Commentary*, 46, No. 3 (September 1968), 86-89.

Views *Morning Noon and Night* as an extension of the mannerisms
and attitudes of *By Love Possessed ;* the latter's style was "affected,
overblown, frequently clumsy in construction, far from any
idiom of actual human speech, and loaded with grotesque redun-
dancies and gratuitous ornaments." Thompson also finds fault
with the tone of *By Love Possessed,* which is such that it is impossible to believe that Arthur Winner is not being set up for
disaster–and there is none. The style was "a bold endeavor
to pit rhetoric against the whole plain sense of his story, to
use a baroque, outlandish, and even offensive style to try and
give weight and complication to a tale he might with more
consonance have told in the simple, craftsmanlike manner of
some of his previous well-observed and well-ordered novels."
The effect is that "it resembles perhaps a mock-epic style, in
which insignificant acts . . . are described with the rhetoric and
machinery normally reserved for imperial themes, and the result
is comic. But Cozzens's view of his story could not withstand
the comic . . . and so he employed a baroque irony, a kind
of insurance or hedging that now inflates, now deflates, and
avoids the responsibility of ever saying just what scale these
figures should have." Cozzens' view is just as ambiguous in
Morning Noon and Night, but here the uncertainty becomes a
tiresome puzzle. Moreover, instead of irony at human passion
and folly, all that *Morning Noon and Night* has to offer is "disgust,
guilt, and contempt." Thompson's belief is that Cozzens "has
meant to give a portrait of a cold-hearted, conceited, ruthless
man, whose acts and beliefs would grate most raspingly on the
sensibilities of many readers; and he meant to indicate his great
admiration for everything this man stands for. What he did not
know . . . is how successfully the drawling, relentless irony, the
infatuated "literary' posings, the half-ironic echoing, echoing,
echoing everywhere of literary tags and mincing clichés, and the
appalling series of other people's deaths and disasters reported
as if with total indifference here and there among the long
inconsequential musings and character sketches and casually
vicious remarks–Cozzens could not have known how very well

all this would represent the most miserable emptiness of Henry
Dodd Worthington and the worthlessness of the little things
he stands for."

D239 *Time*, 92, No. 9 (August 30, 1968), 63. "Cozzens
Against the Grain."

Cozzens has attempted to write a "severe anti-novel" and the
result is less than successful. The method is "indirect and
discursive, dicey and erratic," the plot is irrational, everything
being presented in fits and starts; the themes are developed and
dropped capriciously. The novel fails "because Cozzens has
chosen to write against the grain of his own special talent–that
of a meticulous and compulsive craftsman."

D240 *Times Literary Supplement* [London], January 30, 1969,
p. 116. "Ponderosity."

The reviewer doubts that the subject of the novel may arouse
interest in the reader, but he mainly objects to the style, which
is a mere "rococo version" of the style of *By Love Possessed*.
"Mr. Cozzens's literary hesitation becomes a stammer, . . . his
ponderosity is contrived to his own satisfaction. . . . The point
of view, presented as H. W.'s (but the author's own ?), has the
merit of singularity; a complex attitude, apparently exposing the
reality beneath pretension while really erecting an entirely
different pretentiousness over the exposure."

D241 Updike, John. "Indifference," *New Yorker*, 44, No. 37
(November 2, 1968), 197-201.

"A prose unique in its mannered ugliness, a monstrous mix of
Sir Thomas Browne, legalese, and Best-Remembered Quotations," which, for descriptive purposes, can best be classified
into "The Unresisted Cliché," "The Lame Echo," "The False
Precision," "The Vapid Expansion," "The Inversion Frightful,
Capped by Cute Periphrasis," "The Gratuitous Scientism,"
and "The Infatuated Sonority." Such style, used to capture

the "all too veritably human quality of *stuffiness*," is unbearable. The very subject of the novel becomes strangely insignificant: "Resigned pessimism is a defensible philosophy, and may be the natural end of American Protestantism, but it makes for very dull fiction."

Index

References are to the secondary sources in which Cozzens' books are mentioned.

Ask Me Tomorrow

A1, A2, A3, A4, A5, B5, B20, B26, C3, C5, C6, C8, C15, C17, C20, C23, C25, C33, C34, C43, C44, C61, C65, C70, C72, C73, D115, D158, D184.
Reviews: D79-D94.

By Love Possessed

A1, A2, A3, A4, A5, B1, B2, B4, B5, B8, B9, B10, B16, B20, B21, B22, B23, B24, B27, B28, C2, C3, C5, C7, C8, C12, C15, C16, C17, C18, C19, C21, C22, C24, C27, C28, C29, C31, C32, C33, C34, C35, C36, C37, C38, C39, C40, C43, C44, C46, C47, C54, C55, C56, C58, C59, C61, C62, C64, C65, C66, C67, C70, C72, C73, D196, D201, D204, D207, D208, D215, D218, D221, D224, D226, D228, D229, D231, D232, D236, D238.
Reviews: D132-D192

Castaway

A1, A2, A3, A4, A5, B1, B6, B10, B18, B20, B24, B26, C3, C8, C12, C13, C20, C25, C26, C27, C31, C34, C36, C42, C44, C69, C70, C73, D33, D152, D160.
Reviews: D50-D58.

Children and Others

A2, A4, C58
Reviews: D193-D218

Cock Pit

A1, A2, A3, A4, B24, C8, C15, C25, C34, C61, D20.
Reviews: D8-D11

Confusion

A1, A2, A4, B24, B26, C8, C15, C25, C34, C61, C65, C68, C70, C72,
D148, D152.
Reviews: D1-D5

Guard of Honor

A1, A2, A3, A4, A5, B1, B2, B5, B7, B8, B10, B12, B13, B15, B16,
B18, B19, B20, B21, B22, B24, B25, B26, B27, B29, C1, C3, C4, C5,
C6, C7, C8, C9, C11, C12, C14, C15, C17, C19, C20, C23, C25,
C27, C30, C31, C32, C33, C34, C35, C37, C43, C44, C49, C53, C58,
C59, C61, C65, C70, C72, C73, D133, D143, D146, D150, D158,
D159, D164, D173, D184, D196, D215, D224, D229, D231, D232,
D239.
Reviews: D112-D131

The Just and the Unjust

A1, A2, A3, A4, A5, B2, B5, B8, B10, B15, B18, B20, B24, B25, B26,
C3, C4, C5, C6, C7, C8, C12, C15, C17, C19, C20, C23, C25, C27,
C31, C34, C35, C43, C44, C58, C61, C65, C66, C68, C69, C70,
C72, C73, C74, D133, D146, D149, D158, D173, D183, D190, D196,
D231, D239.
Reviews: D95-D111

The Last Adam

A1, A2, A3, A4, A5, B1, B5, B8, B10, B16, B20, B21, B24, B25, B26,
C3, C4, C7, C8, C12, C15, C17, C19, C20, C22, C23, C25, C26,
C27, C31, C34, C36, C37, C43, C44, C52, C58, C60, C61, C65, C69,
C70, C72, C73, D64, D77, D99, D108, D133, D149, D160, D183,
D184, D231, D241
Reviews: D35-D49

Men and Brethren

A1, A2, A3, A4, A5, B1, B2, B3, B4, B5, B8, B10, B20, B25, B26, C3, C4, C6, C7, C8, C12, C15, C17, C19, C20, C23, C25, C31, C32, C34, C35, C37, C43, C44, C58, C60, C61, C65, C66, C72, D133, D160, D169, D184, D232.
Reviews: D59-D78

Michael Scarlett

A1, A2, A3, A4, B24, C8, C25, C34, C42, C61, C65, D19
Reviews: D6-D7

Morning Noon and Night

A4, C51
Reviews: D219-D241

S.S. San Pedro

A1, A2, A3, A4, A5, B1, B10, B14, B20, B24, B25, B26, C3, C5, C6, C7, C8, C12, C20, C23, C25, C27, C31, C34, C42, C44, C58, C60, C70, D35, D99, D152, D160, D207, D231
Reviews: D23-D34

The Son of Perdition

A1, A2, A3, A4, B20, B24, C8, C15, C25, C30, C34, C44, C61, C70, D25, D169.
Reviews: D12-D22

Printed by Erasmus Ltd Ghent/Belgium